Bia

To one of the most
beautiful people I've
ever known (inside and out).

Happy Birthday my
favourite Aquarius! ♡

Love always, Sim
2024
Los Angeles

TAROT
A TO Z

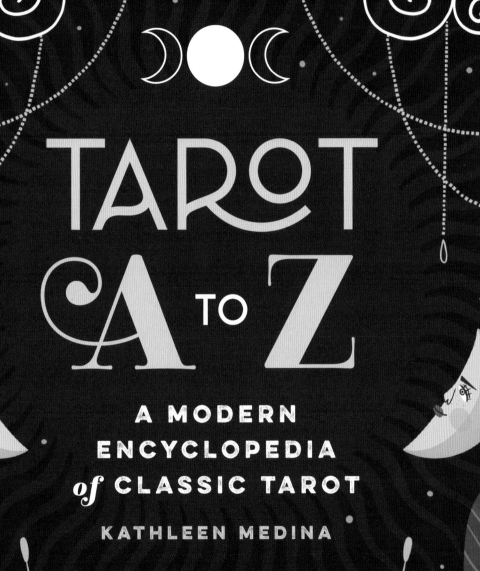

TAROT
A TO Z

A MODERN ENCYCLOPEDIA
of CLASSIC TAROT

KATHLEEN MEDINA

CASTLE POINT BOOKS
NEW YORK

www.castlepointbooks.com

The Castle Point Books trademark is owned by Castle Point Publishing, LLC.
Castle Point books are published and distributed by St. Martin's Publishing Group.

ISBN 978-1-250-28701-4 (hardcover)
ISBN 978-1-250-28702-1 (ebook)

Edited by Jennifer Calvert
Design by Melissa Gerber
Images used under license by Shutterstock.com and Creative Market

Our books may be purchased in bulk for promotional, educational, or business use.
Please contact your local bookseller or the Macmillan Corporate and Premium Sales
Department at 1-800-221-7945, extension 5442, or by email at
MacmillanSpecialMarkets@macmillan.com.

First Edition: 2023

10 9 8 7 6 5 4 3 2 1

THIS BOOK IS DEDICATED TO
ALL THOSE SEEKING ANSWERS
FROM THE UNSEEN REALMS.

Contents

WELCOME TO

TAROT
A TO Z!

Whether you're just beginning to explore Tarot or you wish to deepen your existing knowledge and practice, you've come to the right place. This book is designed for everyone. With a clear overview of the practice, easy-to-understand card interpretations, and a complete encyclopedia of Tarot terms, *Tarot A to Z* can help you tap into your inner wisdom and gain the insight you need to accurately guide yourself and others.

Don't worry if you don't have a deck of your own yet. You can delight in and learn from the soulful imagery that accompanies this book as you explore Tarot—an invaluable divination tool handed down through the ages to awaken your own inner knowing. And don't be intimidated by Tarot's history. This process is going to be fun and exciting. With a straightforward, modern perspective on this ancient, mystical wisdom, you'll learn to approach Tarot pragmatically and simply.

You were drawn to this book for a reason. Maybe you just wanted something fun to do on your Saturday wine-and-cheese nights with your besties. Or maybe you're a seasoned practitioner seeking to deepen your study. No matter what brought you here, you'll find everything you need within the pages of *Tarot A to Z* to make your Tarot practice your own.

How Can Tarot Help?

Knowledge is power, and Tarot is a terrific tool for gaining knowledge that leads to self-awareness. Want to know how to land your dream job? Or why your partner keeps repeating that annoying pattern of behavior? Maybe you just want to step fully into the person you're meant to be. No matter what answers you're seeking, Tarot can help you find them.

In *Tarot A to Z*, you'll immerse yourself in the structure of Tarot, the meaning of each card, the placements, and how to synthesize (read) a spread of cards to decipher its overall guidance. You'll also uncover ways to access your intuition. Combined with understanding the cards and their relationship to each other, your inner guidance system can provide profound illumination.

This practice will help you gain a better understanding of both your conscious mind and your subconscious influences (the underlying reasons you're doing what you're doing). And when you understand the root cause of a problem, the solution presents itself. The cards can point you toward possibilities and even reveal your future trajectory based on where you are in your life at any moment. In other words, Tarot reading gives you a road map for how to move forward.

Who Am I?

As your guide on this journey, I'd like to introduce myself and share my background regarding Tarot. I come from an eclectic family steeped in all things mystical, and I'm a descendant of a line of psychic women on my maternal side. My grandmother was a charismatic Catholic who saw visions, talked with angels and saints, and was a great devotee of Mother Mary. She married a Jewish man who believed in the esoteric power of numbers. (He also studied mathematics.) My three aunts all have intuitive abilities, including energy healing, medical and forensic clairvoyance, and reading Tarot.

✳ MY FIRST READING ✳

As a child, I could hear and see apparitions, which scared me to death. (Imagine a less dramatic version of the kid in *The Sixth Sense*.) I had extrasensory perception regarding people and places. One summer, when I was eleven or twelve, we visited my aunt who read Tarot. I begged her to do a reading; I was fascinated by these enigmatic cards. She finally relented and laid out a large spread. The central theme was The Tower. For those familiar with The Tower, you know this is a challenging signifier (and a very frightening image!). It represents the breakdown of an outworn structure—a healing crisis—often producing anxiety as it's occurring. But it's a necessary storm that clears what doesn't serve the highest good.

I knew immediately what it meant: my family was breaking up. I'd sensed the tension between my parents for quite some time and felt that something was not right in the household, even though my parents put up a front that all was well. (Kids always know the truth, even if they don't under-stand the details.) A year later, my parents divorced, and life as I knew it changed. I found out years later that my aunt had also read my mother's and brother's cards, and The Tower was a central theme for them as well.

✳ MY JOURNEY TO TAROT ✳

Even though it was a difficult introduction to Tarot, my fascination only grew. I bought my first deck of Rider-Waite Tarot (considered the classic Tarot deck and one of the few decks available at the time) when I was fifteen. I began to study and practice, and, over the course of a decade, I started reading for friends. My mother encouraged me to read professionally, but I didn't feel ready.

When I was in my mid-twenties, I went to massage school—a yearlong intensive program in Hawaii. Not only did I learn anatomy, physiology, and massage techniques there, I also learned how to work with energy. We studied the ancient Hawaiian lomilomi massage and basic Huna practices for balancing energy. I learned how to "connect, ground, protect," a simple but powerful process of connecting to Source (your higher self), sending "roots" into the earth to ground yourself, and visualizing yourself encapsulated in white light (a process you can learn more about on page 33). Practitioners of Reiki also use this technique. This was a game changer for me.

I saw the difference this practice made with my massage clients. My heightened awareness gave me a deeper understanding of the issues that were creating blockages in the body, and that made my massages more effective. I soon realized that I could also use this technique to help me with my Tarot readings. Connecting to Source had opened my awareness to a greater capacity. I could consciously turn up the volume on my sensitivity to do a reading and turn down the volume when it was done. Once I trusted that I had some control over the process, I felt ready to start doing readings professionally.

✳ GETTING HERE ✳

My first gig was at a small café in Sydney, Australia. I'd convinced the owner (who was American, like me) to let me sit at a table at the front of the restaurant for a couple of nights. We put out a sandwich-board sign that read, "Tarot: $10 for 10 minutes."

The first night, I had six customers, which I considered a great success. The second night, there was a line out the door, and I did twenty readings. Soon I was doing readings at local metaphysical shops and private parties. I was even hired to do readings for the afterparty of the premiere of *The Matrix.* (Unfortunately, Keanu wasn't there.) During my four years in Australia, I began teaching Tarot classes and developed a curriculum to make it user-friendly.

After returning to the U.S., I found work as a reader at a high-end spa in Santa Fe, New Mexico, before moving to Tucson to join the metaphysical team at Canyon Ranch. I eventually transferred to the Canyon Ranch in Lenox, Massachusetts, where I currently reside. Over the years, I've developed a consistent private practice and now work mostly via phone or Zoom. However, my great love is working with groups and teaching others about Tarot.

In my twenty-five years of professional experience working with clients and students, I've seen how using the cards to facilitate intuition can offer profound guidance. And it's accessible to everyone! You don't have to hail from a psychic line, or grow up around metaphysics, or become an energy healer to be able to read Tarot. When given a chance and taught some basic tools, people can uncover astounding abilities—many surpassing my own. Are you ready to find out more about yours?

PART 1

AN OVERVIEW of TAROT

The Basics of Tarot

Over the centuries, Tarot has been feared and misunderstood, labeled as something dark or occult. But, at its essence, Tarot is a book of symbolism. The cards are archetypal; they contain ancient wisdom, but they don't have a magical power of their own. They're a tool for guidance, helping to open the mind of the reader. This compilation of seventy-eight cards is illustrated with pictures, numbers, and elements to create a symbolic language that stimulates the intuitive, creative side of the brain. Every symbol is there to teach and to give information so we can access greater awareness. Anyone can use this divination tool to gain objectivity and awareness, and to help them understand the nature of a situation. And no reading is set in stone.

✳ THE IMAGERY ✳

The imagery on each of Tarot's seventy-eight cards is designed to evoke a sensation, to open a portal to your intuition—very much like a great work of art. When you look at a painting like Leonardo da Vinci's *Mona Lisa*, for example, a feeling arises—a sense about the mystery of an enigmatic smile that hints at feminine power.

Tarot cards have the same effect. The imagery taps into our fundamental consciousness. Symbols convey a depth of feeling and insight into our lives that is often confounding to the rational analytical mind. But when we activate our intuition (and you will learn how to do that), our minds can open to inner guidance and transcendent knowing.

No matter a deck's subject or design—and you'll find plenty of them on the market—its imagery will speak to the same universal themes of Tarot. The core meaning of each card applies, regardless of which deck you choose to work with. In Part 2 (starting on page 36), we'll go over some of the traditional imagery of the major arcana cards to give you a foundational understanding that you can apply to any deck.

As a Tarot practitioner for more than thirty years, I've used many different types of decks. When working with students and clients, I let them choose the style of deck that resonates with them. A cat lover may choose *Tarot of the Cat People*, a gardener may choose *The Herbal Tarot*, and a traditionalist and lover of medieval iconography may choose *The Rider-Waite Tarot*. Choosing a deck with imagery that speaks to you is simply a way to make your Tarot practice your own.

Oracle Decks

With its ancient origins and complexity based on numbers, elements, and symbolism, Tarot is a unique system with precise building blocks. Oracle cards are different. Often created by authors in the mind/body/spirit world, these popular decks come in a variety of formats and themes (such as animals, angels, or healing). Oracle cards can be very helpful as a tool of contemplation and guidance, but they don't offer the same level of insight as Tarot does.

✳ THE STRUCTURE ✳

You can find innumerable variations of Tarot with different styles and imagery according to the artist's taste and interpretation, but the framework remains the same; Tarot itself is designed with a definitive structure. And when you understand the overall pattern and makeup of a Tarot deck, learning the cards is quite straightfor-ward. Each deck is made up of seventy-eight cards split into two categories: the major arcana and the minor arcana. The twenty-two cards of the major arcana represent overarching themes you may encounter on life's path. The fifty-six cards of the minor arcana give you specific information about particular situations and people. The minor cards are further organized into four suits, representing each of the four elements: earth, air, fire, and water. Each suit contains numbers one (ace) through ten as well as four court cards: page, knight, queen, and king. As long as a deck has this structure, it's a Tarot deck—even if it's covered in colorful kittens or your favorite movie charac-ters. And by working through this structure step-by-step, we'll create the foundation for your own unique Tarot practice.

✳ THE STORY IT TELLS ✳

Once you have your deck, try this little exercise. Separate out the major arcana. Starting with The Fool (0) and ending with The World (XXI), lay out all the cards in numeric order to make a circle. Step back and observe the cards, and you'll see a story unfold. The Fool represents new beginnings, The World represents completion, and the cards in between represent various themes we encounter in life. As you follow this circle, what thoughts arise? Does a certain card jump out at you? If so, pick it up and let the imagery speak to you. What attracts you to it? What feelings stir?

Now separate the minor arcana into the four suits. Make a column for each suit—four columns total—beginning with the aces at the bottom and ending with the kings at the top. The aces show the seed energy of each suit. The kings represent the culmination. Even before understanding the meaning of the elements and numbers, do you glimpse the elegance of the sequence of each suit?

The point of this exercise is threefold: First, it breaks down Tarot into smaller sections so it doesn't seem so overwhelming. Second, it gives you a visual understanding of the overall pattern of a Tarot deck and the stories it can tell. And third, it helps you begin to tap into your intuition and your creative mind. All of this will help you on your Tarot journey.

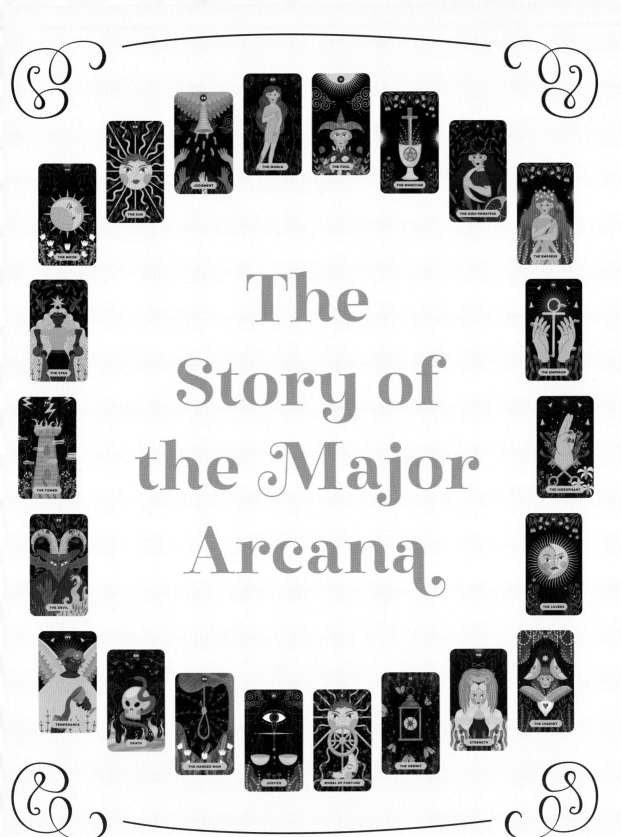

The Story of the Major Arcana

The History of Tarot

The origins of Tarot are shrouded in mystery. Some believe this esoteric deck of cards came from ancient Egypt. Others believe it traveled from northern India to Europe with the Romani people. What we do know is that modern Tarot can be traced back at least as far as the fifteenth century. But we can certainly feel in today's cards the influences of both the early Mystery Schools of Egypt and the mystical Western societies that were later built upon them.

Contributing to Tarot's enigma is the fact that the Catholic Church condemned the cards as heretical in the fifteenth century, driving the practice underground. (*Occult* actually means *hidden*.) Even the playing cards that largely emerged in the Renaissance were forbidden. But during the Age of Enlightenment in the seventeenth century, the use of Tarot as a divination tool flourished. There was renewed interest in esoteric traditions as people began to look to spiritualism, divination, and ancient wisdom for answers.

People continue to explore these practices today, although the shadow of fear of the occult that overlays Tarot remains. And the Catholic Church continues to demonize Tarot, astrology, and other forms of direct inquiry with the Divine. But there is nothing dark about this divination tool. Tarot merely gives us a powerful symbolic language that can open us up to a deeper consciousness, bringing more awareness and objectivity to the many changes and challenges we all face in life.

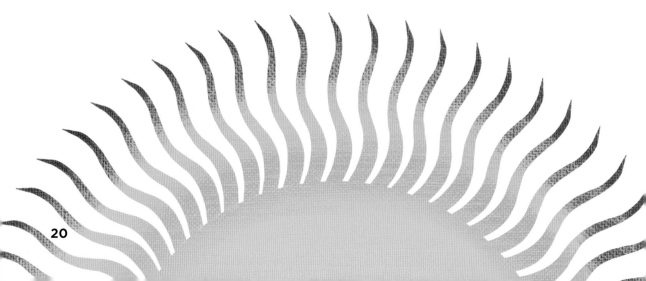

The Egyptian Theory

Some believe Tarot originated in Egypt as a book of wisdom that was taught in the Mystery Schools there. At some point before the first century AD, so the theory goes, the book was separated into cards to be used as a divination tool. And those cards made their way to Europe through travel and conquests. The fact that Egyptians used pictures to communicate complex ideas, and that hieroglyphics predate letters of an alphabet, helps make this a compelling theory.

✳ THE ART OF PLAYING CARDS ✳

Although we don't yet know where Tarot truly originated, historians have traced elements of modern decks back to hand-painted playing cards in the fifteenth century. One of the oldest of these was the Mamluk deck, which comprised four suits with ten numbered cards and three court cards each. This deck and its rich cultural heritage spread across southern Europe with the movement of Islamic forces across North Africa and into the Iberian Peninsula.

Compelling evidence suggests that the use of cards blossomed due to the advent of the printing press in Europe as well as a renewed interest in art and spirituality during the Renaissance. Card games were extremely popular in Italy, with wealthy families commissioning artists to paint decks in their likeness. In fact, the oldest surviving playing cards in existence come from decks belonging to the Visconti family, rulers of Milan. Italians used these decks, which included beautifully illustrated themes (called *trionfi*, or *trumps*), to play a card game called *Tarocco*, or Tarot in English.

One of these decks, the Tarot de Marseille, comprised the same structure as modern decks—fifty-six minor cards and twenty-two major cards. Despite its French name, the deck featured Italian artwork and is thought to have been created in Milan in the mid-1400s. From there, it spread to France, where divination became a common practice in the 1700s.

A Family Affair

Philippe Camoin—a descendant of Nicolas Conver, master card-maker, engraver, and creator of a famous Tarot deck based on the Tarot de Marseille in 1760—collaborated in the 1990s with Alejandro Jodorowsky, and their research has unearthed some interesting findings. Most historians believe Tarot cards emerged in the fifteenth century. However, Camoin and Jodorowsky believe they have evidence to show that the complete Tarot has existed since the first century. After comparing original cards from different periods, Camoin added all European Tarot decks to a database and used Photoshop to reconstruct and layer them on top of each other. He uncovered what he believes to be an original deck with complex motifs laid out with mathematical precision, suggesting there was a prototype on which all future decks were based.

✳ BECOMING TAROT ✳

Both the Mamluk and Italian decks contributed to the creation of Tarot decks, but it took several centuries for Tarot to gain traction openly as a divination practice. We turn to France in the late 1700s to find the earliest known guidebook to Tarot, written by Jean-Baptise Alliette under the pseudonym Etteilla. The book preceded a deck of his own creation—the first in this era designed specifically for the purpose of divination. It was at this time that the Tarot de Marseille, which is still used today, also found use in divination circles.

These earlier decks led to the creation of the well-known Thoth and Rider-Waite decks. In 1898, Aleister Crowley became a member of the Hermetic Order of the Golden Dawn, an English Rosicrucian Society (community of mystics) with roots in the Mystery Schools of antiquity. Crowley's Thoth deck, with art by Egyptologist Lady Frieda Harris, was published in 1969 and clearly shows a relationship with both Egyptian iconography and Jewish mysticism (Kabbalah). It features close to 1,200 symbols, including astrological glyphs and Hebrew letters. It's interesting to note that there are twenty-two letters in the Hebrew alphabet and twenty-two numbers in the major arcana, and that twenty-two is called the "Master Builder" in numerology.

A. E. Waite and illustrator Pamela Colman Smith were also members of the Hermetic Order of the Golden Dawn. Together, they published the Rider-Waite deck in 1909 with publisher William Rider & Son of London. Waite intended the deck to be sold commercially, drawing new practitioners to Tarot. Sometimes called the Smith-Waite or Rider-Waite-Smith deck to give much-deserved credit to its illustrator, it remains one of the most popular decks today and continues to spawn countless interpretations itself.

Symbolism and Tarot

With the understanding that Tarot is essentially a book of symbolism, it's important to look at the profound meaning of symbolism itself. Symbols convey a depth of information not normally accessible to the logical, analytical mind. Imagery, archetypes, and patterns awaken us to the underlying meaning and order of the Universe.

Brilliant psychoanalyst Carl Jung developed the theory of the collective unconscious, a realm of awareness that all humans share. All memories, dreams, and visions, he argued, stem from this collective awareness. Jung posited that archetypes (typical patterns of images and characters) are present in all cultures, and that myths and stories from all societies share a common foundation. It's easy to find cultures throughout history that share similar mythology despite being completely isolated from each other. That's because archetypes emerge from a field of awareness that all people share—the collective unconscious.

Over time and with geographical differences, the development of each culture becomes individualized, and specific eras evolve. But the primal archetypes and themes remain the same. Think of it like a Shakespearean play: over the last 400 years, the characters and parts have remained the same but have been portrayed differently by diverse actors wearing various costumes. This is true of all of us. Our ancestry, genetic makeup, and social conditioning all play a part in our sense of self, but basic archetypes (the loner, the warrior, the nurturer) underlie our nature.

When we work with symbols and archetypes in Tarot, we're going beyond the rational mind and accessing the realm of the collective unconscious. The imagery and patterns in the cards speak to us, providing insight and information that expand our normal awareness. The Universe is always communicating with us; guiding us through synchronicities, numbers, and thematic patterns; and drawing us into a greater comprehension of our potential. Tarot gives us a way to listen and understand—we just need to realize that the mundane and the metaphysical are two sides of the same coin.

Most people don't look beyond the mundane—meaning what we experience with our five senses in the physical world. But every sense and situation have energetic

Meaningful Dreams

Symbolism also plays out in our dreams. In Jungian dream work, interpretation is based on knowledge of the archetypes and patterns inherent in the human condition. During sleep, while our conscious mind is resting, the subconscious has access to the superconscious, which stores the collective overarching messages that can be recorded and understood upon waking. These guide us to our deeper longings, fears, and desires, which are normally not accessible to our conditioned, rational minds.

equivalents: the metaphorical underlying the literal. When we see this, we glimpse a deeper reality, and life, with all its up and downs, starts to feel magical. Aren't we all craving more magic? (Based on the phenomenal success of the *Harry Potter* series, I'd say so!) The study of Tarot can awaken our awareness to the magical, to a world where archetypes come alive to guide us and the wealth of symbols from the collective consciousness are waiting for all who seek them.

Your Inner Guidance System

We all have an inner guidance system; it's part of our sensory—or more precisely, *extrasensory*—perception. People pick up on much more information than they realize. We walk into a room and get a bad feeling about it, or we meet someone and feel an instant connection without knowing why. Think about your own experiences. How many times have you gotten a feeling about something and brushed it off? How often did you regret it? These perceptions don't make sense to the rational mind because they're coming from a different part of the brain (the right hemisphere, which governs intuition and creativity). But that doesn't mean they aren't valid.

Everyone is intuitive—*everyone*. But in Western culture especially, people tend to value the logical, rational, analytical mind (the left hemisphere of the brain) more than their intuition. We aren't taught to listen to or develop the intuitive aspect of ourselves. Thankfully, intuition is a muscle that we can strengthen. The more we learn to trust this inner guidance, the stronger it gets. And the stronger it gets, the more we're willing to trust it.

Working with the cards will help, but focusing first on strengthening your intuition will help it develop free from outside influences. Plus, a stronger sense of intuition will deepen your readings. (That's why we're starting here!) With a better understanding of how your intuition works and a few simple exercises to help it along, you'll learn to access your inner guidance system with ease.

Decoding the Symbolism

When we interpret the cards, we employ both the logical side of the brain and the collective unconscious to help us glean the deeper messages inherent in Tarot. That's why, alongside the descriptions of the major arcana cards (starting on page 48), you'll find breakdowns of their symbolic themes. Learning to see the whole picture, one card at a time, will help you build a foundation for future readings.

❋ CLAIRSENTIENCE, CLAIRAUDIENCE, CLAIRVOYANCE ❋

There are three main ways intuition speaks to us: clairsentience, clairaudience, and clairvoyance. The most predominant is clairsentience, which means *clear feeling*. This is the gut instinct, that inner knowing. It's something you sense and feel in the body. Say, as a parent, you drop your child off at school and go to work. In the middle of the day, you keep getting a feeling that something has happened with your child. Then, when you pick them up, you find out they skinned their knee on the playground after lunch and had to go to the nurse to get patched up. That's clairsentience.

Clairaudience means *clear hearing*. It's that voice inside your head—not the droning inner critic or the running commentary of your mind, but the small, soft voice that whispers guidance. It may say something like, "Call John," a person you haven't talked to for a while and just thought of out of the blue. So you pick up the phone and call John, who says, "This is amazing. I was just thinking of you!" And you have a wonderful conversation.

The most famous of the three ways of receiving intuitive guidance is clairvoyance, or *clear seeing*. Clairvoyance happens in the mind's eye. It is intuition coming to you through a visual medium such as colors, symbols, or quick flashes of a scene. Most professional psychics and mediums are clairvoyant.

Real Clairvoyance

In the movies and on TV, we often see overdramatized examples of psychics having visions. The psychic is suddenly stopped in their tracks by scenes that take over their mind. In reality, clairvoyance can be much more subtle. The visions are often metaphorical rather than literal—the person having the vision receives symbolic mental images that they have to then translate into guidance. For example, an image of a hand holding out a red rose flashes in the mind's eye. This might be a symbol of romantic love being offered rather than an actual scene that's yet to happen.

✳ RECOGNIZING YOUR INTUITION ✳

So, how do you know if it's your intuition speaking and not your everyday thoughts? It just takes practice. As you strengthen your intuition, your impressions will get clearer, and the difference between your thoughts and your inner guidance will become more and more obvious. But understanding how the two differ can help.

The most important distinction between your thoughts and intuition is that intuition is always neutral—meaning there's no emotion attached to it. We can rarely say the same for our thoughts! Intuitive guidance is never judgmental, insecure, arrogant, or fearful. That means that any feelings of self-doubt, worry, or agitation are not your intuition speaking—those belong to your rational mind. Now, you may certainly have emotional *responses* to your intuition. In fact, you can count on it. You'll find your rational mind saying, "What?!" But your intuition itself doesn't carry an emotional charge—it's simply sensory information.

In addition to being neutral, intuitive flashes are also typically so brief that most people miss them. The mind's chatter, however, tends to be louder and more persistent. Our thoughts, fantasies, and desires are well established and easy to recognize. We typically think the same thoughts over and over, which makes those habitual thinking patterns familiar territory.

The brain is like a computer; it can only analyze the data we put into it. And it'll do that over and over, trying to find new answers to old problems. Without giving it new data to go on, that's an impossible task. By listening to your intuition, you're accessing new information. That requires turning down the volume on the rational, analytical mind and turning up the volume on the subtle senses (aka your intuition).

✳ QUIETING THE MIND ✳

If our inner guidance is always available and always speaking to us, why don't we always hear it? This is a common question with a simple answer: the constant chatter of our minds is drowning it out. The first thing you need to do to tap into your intuition is quiet your mind. You need to stop the running commentary in your brain long enough to perceive something else.

Meditation is one practice that's well known for quieting the mind. It also reduces stress, promotes inner peace and awareness, helps manage pain, and aids neurological and cardiovascular function. With so many positive effects, it's certainly worth a try!

The essence of meditation is focusing your awareness on your breath, a mantra (a repeating word or phrase), or a visualization (an image you hold in your mind). By focusing your mind, you quiet the chatter and let your inner voice shine through. And you don't need to spend an hour a day sitting on a cushion to see results. There are plenty of simple things you can do for just a few minutes at a time to achieve a quieter state of mind. Let's start with the basics:

- **Deep breathing:** Deep breathing promotes an almost instant shift from agitation to calmness. Try it: take three long, deep breaths, inhaling through the nose and exhaling through the mouth. Do you notice a shift? Do you feel a bit calmer?

- **Mantras:** Repeating a word or phrase either out loud or in your mind changes your pattern of thinking. The word "peace" repeated a few times can actually help you feel more peaceful. (This is the reverse of what many of us do, which is to repeat a fearful thought over and over and then wonder why we're anxious!)

- **Visualization:** This simple practice involves holding a beautiful image in your mind's eye. Close your eyes and focus on an image that calms you or that you hope to bring into reality. Then lift the corners of your mouth into a gentle smile and take a deep breath. Voilà! You've just practiced the art of creative visualization, which both quiets your mind and helps you manifest more positivity in your life. (You can also do this exercise by gazing downward at something beautiful, such as flowers or a photo of a serene environment.)

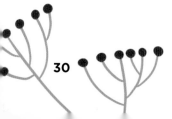

A Long Track Record

We have a variety of meditation practices available to us today, but the origins of meditative practice are ancient—meditation has been part of Hindu tradition for 5,000 years! And all spiritual traditions have some sort of meditative or contemplative practice. Think of the medicine man staring at a candle flame or a medium gazing into a crystal ball. Quieting the mind to receive information from a higher source is and always has been a universal practice.

Monkey Mind

"Monkey mind" is a Buddhist term that describes the uncontrolled mind jumping from one thought to the next. If you take a moment to observe your thoughts, you'll see that they are like little monkeys hopping from tree to tree in the rainforest. You need to get those monkeys to settle down so you can hear your intuition speak.

✴ PAYING ATTENTION ✴

Now that we have a few techniques under our belt, we can move to the next step: paying attention. Let's start with a quick exercise that can help. All you need is a pen and paper. (You may even want to invest in a journal where you can write down your perceptions—your intuition notebook.) The steps are simple:

1. **Take three deep breaths.** Now write down ten sense perceptions. What do you feel in your body? Maybe you notice tension in your neck or feelings of hunger. Do you notice any emotions? Are you tired? Excited? Worried?

2. **Take another deep breath.** Now write down ten things you hear in your environment. Someone talking in the next room? Traffic noise? Birds singing? Also listen internally. Is there a song in your head? A thought that keeps repeating itself? Write it down.

3. **Take another deep breath.** This time, write down ten things you see. Try using your peripheral vision by keeping your focus on the paper but writing what you observe around you. (It's easier to perceive energy when using peripheral vision.) Now close your eyes and note any fleeting images that come across your mind's eye. Colors? Pictures of objects? A certain person?

After another deep breath, take a look at what you wrote. When you read over your sense perceptions of feeling, hearing, and seeing, do you notice any themes? Maybe you had a feeling of calmness, heard the gentle rain, and saw your cat sleeping next to you. Or you had a sense of being rushed, heard the clock ticking, and saw an image of racing in your car to your next appointment in your mind's eye. There are no right or wrong answers, and there may not be any obvious patterns. This is simply a practice of noticing what you are perceiving. From there, it's only another small step to tapping into your intuition and noticing its subtler messages.

✳ CONNECT, GROUND, PROTECT ✳

A great way to connect with your higher self, or Source energy, and amplify your intuition is through another easy exercise called "connect, ground, protect." This is a mini meditation you can use anytime, anywhere. It only takes a moment. Use "connect, ground, protect" whenever you need extra energy and clarity, or when you need to quiet your mind and realign.

It's a simple process: Imagine a column of white light descending from above, encapsulate yourself within it, then send it deep into the earth below you. And if you're not a visual person and find it difficult to visualize the light, you can just think the words *connect*, *ground*, *protect*. By connecting to the light and grounding the light, it becomes protective against lower energies. This exercise also opens your field of awareness to help you perceive intuitive guidance more easily. It may sound too simplistic, or like magical thinking, but try it and see what happens.

Sending Energy to Others

You can also use the "connect, ground, protect" practice to help others. Imagine seeing someone in line at the grocery store who's struggling—they're at the checkout counter taking a long time, digging through a large bag to find the money they mindlessly threw in there earlier. Most of us would just stand there, feeling irritated, but there's another option: you can send them some helpful energy. You never know what someone is going through or how much a little positive energy can help. It's not invasive, and it doesn't mess with anyone's free will. It's just an energetic form of prayer—you're praying for divine Source energy to help somebody instead of complaining about the person in your head. Simply see them connected, grounded, and protected in their own column of light.

☀ HONING YOUR INTUITION ☀

Now let's try another quick exercise, focusing our attention inward this time. Grab your paper (or intuition notebook) and pen, and sit with your back straight and feet on the floor, if possible. Start with the "connect, ground, protect" exercise on page 33 to help you clear your mind and connect with your higher self. Then follow these steps:

1. Take three deep breaths and close your eyes, turning your attention inward to your body. What sensations do you notice? Scan your body and note any feelings that arise. Write down the first five things you perceive.

2. Take another deep breath and close your eyes again, turning your attention inward to what you hear (mentally this time). What sounds or words come to your mind? What thoughts arise? Write down the first five things you hear.

3. Take another deep breath and close your eyes again. What images arise in your mind's eye? A flash of a person, symbol, or scene? Write down the first five things you see.

This exercise requires you to sit back within yourself and allow space for intuition. These sensations will come very quickly, so don't think! Just perceive and note. The subtler senses are quieter and more fleeting than our normal sense perceptions. The key is to be an observer, a witness to what arises—you can think about it later.

When you're done, put down the pen, close your eyes, and take a deep breath. Quiet your mind and focus your attention. Now come back to what you wrote during the exercise. Does anything jump out at you? Is there any kind of pattern or connection between the different subtle sense perceptions? Does a message emerge?

Try completing this exercise every day for a week. (It only takes a few minutes, and the practice quickly becomes second nature.) After a week, you'll be able to look over all that you've written and see some repetition, make some connections, and sense your intuition at work. And you'll discover the predominant way in which your intuition speaks to you. When you bring that knowledge to your Tarot practice, you can discern themes and guidance with deeper clarity.

PART 2

INTERPRETING
the CARDS

The Major Arcana

The major arcana represent overarching life themes. If a spread of cards in your reading has numerous major arcana cards, this is a time in your life when a lot is happening. You're in a big growth phase, which heralds a time of great personal evolution. Depending on the specific cards and their themes, you have an opportunity to understand where you are on your path. Major arcana cards give you a big-picture look at things, the lay of the land. Majors don't indicate specificity in time, but, as a general rule, their effect is felt within six to twelve months. Bigger processes take longer to play out.

The major arcana comprise the core themes of life that begin with The Fool (0) and end with The World (XXI). The Fool is the beginning, the oneness with Source, the leaping-off point. The World characterizes coming full circle, but with greater knowledge and awareness. Each card of the majors is a step on your journey and in your personal evolution in life.

After working with Tarot for a while, you'll notice that certain themes repeat themselves. Some even seem to follow you around. These might be themes that you're still working on or that haven't fully played out yet. They could also represent the core archetypes that reflect your personal life's journey. Everyone has them, and they'll repeat over the course of your life.

The following pages will help you learn more about the major arcana cards and the themes each one represents. But understanding how they reflect or impact your own life requires more than an individual card's interpretation. When you're ready to learn more and synthesize your own readings, you'll find all you need in Part 3: Putting Things into Perspective.

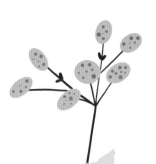

The Minor Arcana

While the twenty-two major arcana cards deal with overarching themes, the fifty-six minor arcana cards deal with specifics. They're indicators of particular events, people, states of mind, and emotions. We look to the minors to get a sense of timing and a better understanding of the area of life indicated by whichever cards come up in a spread. This is why learning the structure of the cards is so important—these are the nuts and bolts of a reading.

Each of the four suits in the minor arcana includes cards numbered from ace (one, the beginning) to ten (the culmination). There are also the sixteen court cards—a page, knight, queen, and king of each suit—that give us insight and information about people and personalities. Most of the time, a reading will include both major and minor cards, and you'll be able to identify key themes. But occasionally, a spread is mostly minor arcana. This just signifies that there are a lot of moving parts at this time in your life. So the devil is in the details! Later in this section, we'll approach learning the fifty-six cards of the minor arcana step-by-step to give you a better understanding of those details.

Getting to Know the Court Cards

Depending on their placement in a spread and their relationship with the other cards, court cards can represent aspects of the reader or of other people. For example, the order of page to king signifies a progression of maturity. Court cards can also signify changing aspects of yourself—the energy you're in for certain periods of time. Figuring out whether a court card in a reading represents your own energy or another person's takes practice. But understanding the elements, the numbers, and the personalities of these cards will go a long way in helping you hone your interpretation of your readings. You'll find profiles on each court card in the pages that follow.

✴ UNDERSTANDING THE SUITS ✴

Each of the four suits represents an area (or areas) of your life, helping you get a clearer understanding of your reading's focus. Wands—a visual symbol of creation—represents the realm of activity, energy, and movement. Pentacles represents the material realm, money, and physicality, which is why it's usually portrayed as coins. Cups, which shows vessels typically illustrated as chalices or goblets, signifies the emotional realm, feelings, and relationships. Swords embodies the realm of thought, ideas, and beliefs. This suit's sharp-edged symbol can indicate conflict or cutting through the noise. Each suit also corresponds to an element (fire, earth, water, and air, respectively), which we'll delve into more in "Factoring in the Elements" on page 43.

✴ TAROT BY THE NUMBERS ✴

Numerology is the esoteric science of numbers, which can be traced back to antiquity. It's based on the numbers one through nine, each of which represents a particular energy and meaning. Understanding the significance of these numbers will bring a lot of insight to your Tarot readings. And you can discover the meaning behind any number, no matter how big it is, using basic math. Simply add its digits until you've reduced them to a single number between one and nine. For example, twenty-three carries the energy of five (two plus three). Although zero and ten aren't core numbers, they deserve honorable mentions. Zero doesn't stand on its own but instead uplifts the energy of other numbers. Ten is an important number in the minor arcana and carries the energy of one and zero. See the box on page 40 for a quick guide to the meaning behind each number.

A Numerology Cheat Sheet

*The following keywords and phrases can
help you get a feeling for the energy of each number. These digits
cover a lot of ground, so look to the rest of your reading for context.*

Zero (0): Source, the Divine, grace, blessings; freedom from limitations, potential, choice

One (1): Beginnings, new energy; independence, learning self-reliance; leadership, pioneering ideas, inspired thought; a need to assert one's will, domineering, stubbornness

Two (2): Harmony, balance, adaptability; relationships, peacemaking, sensitivity to and awareness of others; indecision, timidity

Three (3): Creative expression, beauty, pleasure, luxury, art and design; optimism, positivity; sociability, affable nature, extroversion; gossip and drama

Four (4): Builder of solid foundations; practicality, caution, dependability, organization; orientation toward material items and work; conservative and even miserly tendencies

Five (5): Communication; freedom, travel, movement, adventure, excitement, exploration; scattered energies, restlessness, change

Six (6): Family, love, marriage, home, domesticity; responsibility, service to others, loyalty; smothering nature, overprotectiveness

Seven (7): Introspection, spiritual studies, meditation, knowing the mind; solitude, withdrawal into one's own world; focus on intellectual pursuits, science, research

Eight (8): Power, ambition, wealth, success, business; strong body and mind, drive, courage; materialism, pride

Nine (9): Fruition, culmination, maturation; idealism, humanitarianism, selflessness, generosity, forgiveness; wisdom, old souls, broad concepts; perfectionism, tests

Ten (10): New beginnings, divine grace; transition, renewal, decisions; merging of identities, new challenges from Source

It's no accident that there are twenty-two major arcana cards. In numerology, twenty-two is one of three powerful Master Numbers: eleven, twenty-two, and thirty-three. These numbers with repeating digits amplify the energy of the single digit they embody. Think of a Master Number as an honors class in a particular subject—it takes things up a notch. In the minor arcana, you're only working with one (ace) through ten. The major arcana, however, includes Master Numbers eleven and twenty-two, and it carries the significance of the latter in its structure.

The Master Numbers

Although Master Numbers include all double-digit repeating numbers, eleven, twenty-two, and thirty-three are especially powerful signifiers. These numbers represent greater challenges, but also greater opportunities.

Eleven (11), the Master Intuitive: Prophecy, inspiration, intuition, vision; spiritual, philosophical, and religious leader; fame and/or notoriety

Twenty-two (22), the Master Builder: Hard worker, realization of dreams, creation of structures that help others; executives, large organizations, diplomacy; potential to affect many lives

Thirty-three (33), the Master Teacher: Optimism, creativity, self-expression; communication, compassion, using talents to be of service and help others

Many cultures have used the principles of numerology. Western numerology has its origins in Chaldean and Kabbalah numerology. Kabbalah numerology—part of esoteric Judaism—works with the twenty-two letters of the Hebrew alphabet. Every letter has a sound, a vibration. When letters are put together to make words, that combined vibration then creates a new form with its own energy. And all forms (words) can be traced back to those twenty-two vibrations. So early mystics determined that there were twenty-two core building blocks that could create any form.

The major arcana represent those twenty-two building blocks—the twenty-two themes that comprise the soul's journey on earth. At different points in your life, you'll notice different themes. For example, The Lovers card indicates that a romantic relationship or union with another is in your future. Death heralds profound transformation and letting go of something to make room for something else to emerge. Temperance points to a time of deep psychological understanding, focusing within, gaining greater awareness of your own makeup, and integrating the parts of your nature that you've pushed back into the unconscious (your shadow side).

As you can see, there's a reason for the numeric and thematic structure of the major arcana. But, obviously, the themes don't show up in a reading in the foundational order of zero to twenty-one. The cards that show up in your readings reflect what's intended for you. Understanding the structure just helps you put your reading into perspective.

The Energy of Twenty-Two

Twenty-two is often called the Master Builder, the number of the building blocks of a higher order. This number is influenced by the number four (two plus two), which represents the earth plane: what you experience on the ground, the practical aspects of life, your foundation, your routine, and what sustains you. But four and twenty-two represent two different journeys.

Imagine you inherited a plot of land, a place where you can build a house. In relation to that, the energy of the number four in your reading would signify building something secure and practical to ensure your basic needs of food, clothing, and shelter are met—no frills. The number twenty-two, however, would represent building your dream home. It would signify trusting your intuition (represented by the number two) to create something balanced, harmonious, and beautiful that could provide the foundation for your dreams and the longing of your spirit for a long time to come.

Factoring in the Elements

The four suits of the minor arcana signify four distinct elemental aspects: Swords represents air and thought, Wands represents fire and action, Cups represents water and emotions, and Pentacles represents earth and physicality. These elements are the building blocks of our human experience, the basis of everything in our lives. Understanding a minor arcana card's element is key to understanding its vibration within a reading.

The Ten of Swords in the Rider-Waite deck offers a great example of this. This card features a dead man lying facedown on the ground with ten swords in his back. That's a disturbing image for sure! But this is a Swords card, and Swords represents air, the element of thought. So this card indicates death *of a way of thinking*. Generally, this is good news. But if you don't know the card's element and just go by the image, you might be a little freaked out.

Each of the four elements is also associated with a set of astrological signs (explained in the following pages), adding another layer of information to your readings. In the court cards, this can give you an easy way to understand a person's basic nature—whether that's yours or someone else's. Everyone has a corresponding court card. For example, an Aries woman would be represented by the Queen of Wands. A youngster with a Pisces sun sign would be a Page of Cups. You'll learn more about these representations as we get into the individual cards' meanings starting on page 70.

✳ FIRE ✳

Symbolized by Wands, fire is an element driven by action. This extroverted, masculine energy only feels comfortable if it's moving toward something. It calls you to act, to put your ideas into motion, to move your body. The fire signs of the zodiac—Aries, Leo, and Sagittarius—fit this description perfectly.

- **Aries:** This fiery sign is the spark, the first sign of the fire element. Aries season begins on the vernal equinox (March 20 or 21), which is the first day of spring and the start of the astrological calendar. Ruled by Mars, Aries is a powerful force to initiate something (think spring fever!).

- **Leo:** Leo season is midsummer in the northern hemisphere. This sign, which is ruled by the Sun, is about full expression, shining your light, being fully seen, having an audience, and sharing your gifts. It's a sign of leadership and creativity. Leos have something to say and need to find an arena in which to say it.

- **Sagittarius:** Sagittarius represents effortless movement, be it travel, physical activity, or adventure. Sagittarians want to expand their field of experience, see new lands, meet new people, and stay on the move. These outgoing folks are ruled by Jupiter, a planet associated with expansion, so they're always looking for new opportunities and fields of interest.

✳ EARTH ✳

Represented by Pentacles, earth speaks to all aspects of physicality, health, money, and the material world. This element covers everything happening on the ground. Earth carries a feminine energy representing growth, fertility, the soil, plants, crops, and trees. As the densest element, it moves more slowly as it manifests in the outer world. The signs bringing this grounded energy to life are Taurus, Virgo, and Capricorn.

- **Taurus:** Taurus represents all the beauty and comforts of the material realm, enjoying good food, gardens, and financial security. This sign is ruled by Venus, so think love and money. Sensuous Taureans also appreciate affection and the satisfaction of the physical senses. But as a fixed sign (the least movable of the modalities), Taureans can be stubborn.

- **Virgo:** Virgo is the practical aspect of the earth signs. They're the healer, the helper, and the one who takes care of the details. This sign is ruled by Mercury, the planet of thinking and communication that lends itself to thoughtful productivity. Virgos believe in integrity, doing good work, and taking things one step at a time to ensure everything is done right.

- **Capricorn:** Capricorn is all about taking care of business. This sign likes structure, long-range projects, and building solid foundations. It's a more traditional energy and prefers the tried-and-true ways of being in the world. Ruled by Saturn, the ancient god of time, Capricorn takes the long view. Slow and steady wins the race!

✳ AIR ✳

Illustrated by the suit of Swords, air represents the mental realm, thought, analysis, inspiration, and ideas. This element moves fast, like the speed of thought. Its expression is knowledge, learning, and information. Air is a masculine element, so detachment, rational logic, and operating from the left brain are its milieu. Gemini, Libra, and Aquarius are the quick-thinking air signs.

- **Gemini:** Gemini is ruled by Mercury, the messenger. This planet is closest to the Sun, moving quickly in its orbit. Communication is key to Gemini, be it verbal or written. They need to learn, study, and accumulate information. The Gemini mind is restless! This sign is always looking at their phones, Googling, and posting on social media.

- **Libra:** Libra represents balance. Ruled by Venus, Libra prizes harmony and peace. This sign weighs ideas, deliberates, and seeks win-win solutions so everyone can be happy. Libras are risk- and conflict-averse, always seeking a way to get along with others and keep the peace.

- **Aquarius:** Aquarius is the big brain of the zodiac. This sign is all about thinking outside the box, innovative ideas, and big-picture concepts. Ruled by Uranus, Aquarius is a sign of eccentricity and freedom of thought. Aquarians can be wildly brilliant. Typically, this sign prefers to gather ideas from lots of different sources. The internet, with its seemingly endless web of information, is Aquarius's playground.

☀ WATER ☀

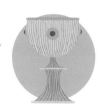

Embodied by the suit of Cups, water is the element of feeling, emotions, and intuition. It's feminine, yin, and fluid—a powerful force that can be very changeable. Think of playing in the small ripples of a calm ocean when a wave seems to come from nowhere and crashes over you. Experiencing life on the ever-changing emotional level is the essence of the water signs: Cancer, Scorpio, and Pisces.

- **Cancer:** Cancer is the nurturer, the mother archetype to Capricorn's father archetype. Family and home are their domain. This sign is always sensitive to others' needs. But Cancerians are also moody and prone to worry. Ruled by the Moon, Cancer's emotions can fluctuate like the tides.

- **Scorpio:** Scorpio represents death, sexuality, and resurrection. This sign is all about deep, intense emotions, but Scorpios often hide their sensitivity in a shell of self-protection. Their secretive nature can make it hard to understand them. Ruled by Pluto, Scorpio is the most powerful sign of the zodiac. Themes of power struggles, the need to use life-force energy in a positive way, and passionate longing make this a truly interesting sign.

- **Pisces:** Pisces, the last sign of the zodiac, is all about the collective unconscious, humanitarianism, and empathy. Pisces is ruled by Neptune, the planet of spirituality and intuition. Incredibly sensitive and psychic, this water sign feels your pain. There's a dreamy, sometimes escapist, element to Pisces because of their heightened sensitivity.

0 · The Fool

THE FOOL

As the first card of the twenty-two cards of the major arcana, The Fool is the card par excellence of new beginnings. It heralds oneness with Source energy and being on the threshold of a grand adventure. When The Fool appears, it is saying you are being guided and you are safe to follow a new path. Now is the time to trust your gut instincts. Jump and the chute will appear!

This card does not indicate "foolishness" in the negative sense. There is an innocence to The Fool, a simplicity. The Fool knows he is being guided and supported. He knows that he is not supposed to understand all the phases of a new journey. His only job is to step off the cliff and start. The Fool calls forth beginner's mind (a mindset of humility and curiosity)— he needs only openness, trust, and faith. The rest will be revealed as he proceeds on his new path. This card offers blessings and grace—the force is with you!

Decoding the Symbolism

With no end or beginning, zero represents the alpha and omega. It is the number of the Divine. In many decks, The Fool stands on the edge of a high cliff with snowcapped mountains in the background. Mountains represent seeking spiritual attainment, oneness with the Divine, and elevated consciousness. He often holds a white rose (a symbol of purity) and carries very little or nothing at all for his journey because he needs only his innocent heart and open consciousness. In many decks, you will see a little dog with him; his instincts are his loyal companion. (It's nice, validating imagery for dog lovers too!)

I · The Magician

A conduit between Heaven and Earth

This card is the first manifest number on the journey. The Magician stands poised between the great unknowable and the earthly plane, the bridge between the realms. He is still connected to Source, receiving guidance, and he is being asked to begin implementing that guidance.

This card signifies communication. You can find a way to channel your inspirations if you listen to them and recognize the need to share them. That might look like speaking up more in certain situations. Or it could mean writing a blog or a book, or even just beginning to journal your thoughts and ideas. Bottom line: your insights are needed. The Magician also indicates that you're in the right place at the right time to share them. Begin to play with the brilliance streaming from within you.

Decoding the Symbolism

The number one is about individuality, initiative, innovation—lots of "i" words! It is a progressive number directed at the future. In many decks, the imagery shows a man with his right hand raised to the sky and his left hand pointed at the ground. He is like a lightning rod, grounding the electricity in the air.

Often, The Magician is portrayed with the four elements: earth, air, fire, and water. This signifies that he has the essential ingredients to begin manifesting his inspirations into form. Sometimes, The Magician is portrayed as the messenger Hermes (aka Mercury). If we think of The Fool as jumping off the cliff, then The Magician has landed. He's telling you it's time to recognize that you've landed where you need to be, whether that's in a certain location, in a new job, or with a burning idea that you are thinking about bringing into reality.

II · The High Priestess

THE HIGH PRIESTESS

The High Priestess is mysterious, confident, and a force unto herself. Emotionally independent, she knows who she is. She is Sophia, the Goddess of wisdom. She is the Oracle at Delphi, sitting regally in the temple, not bothering with the commotion below in the street. And she softly urges you to listen to your inner voice, to trust your intuition, and to consult your own oracle.

The High Priestess signifies a time to withdraw from the noise and retreat to your inner sanctum so you can hear the wisdom within you. She also suggests the feminine power that is born out of the dark and mysterious, that can't be touched or altered. The High Priestess may seem passive, removed, and detached, like she's not doing anything. But she is. She's listening. She knows and trusts her own wisdom, and she asks that you trust yours.

Decoding the Symbolism

The symbolism on The High Priestess card is especially mysterious. She is often portrayed wearing light blue (a color of intuition) and with the moon, indicating the lunar feminine qualities of quiet reflection but also of great power. Remember, the gravitational pull of the moon controls the tides. In the Rider-Waite Tarot deck, she sits in the temple between a black pillar and a white pillar, which indicates a balance of opposites. The High Priestess holds many secrets. She is the guardian of esoteric wisdom. And if you get this card, she is offering to share that wisdom with you.

Because the numbers of the major arcana are in Roman numerals, the number two looks like an eleven. In numerology, eleven means that your spirit is guiding you. And interestingly, this Master Number also reduces to two, which signifies sensitivity, feeling, balance, and intuition. Your inner goddess is in the driver's seat!

III · The Empress

Fertility, creativity, and abundance

The Empress is juicy, juicy, juicy! While The High Priestess embodies inner riches, The Empress represents being surrounded by outer riches. Beautiful and voluptuous, she exudes sensuality and is not embarrassed about enjoying the good life. She calls you to enjoy earthly delights. This card's energy is Venusian, and Venus (Aphrodite) is all about love and money.

THE EMPRESS

The Empress also signifies motherhood, literally and metaphorically. She calls you to give birth to what's inside you. This card tells you it's time to cultivate what you want to be surrounded by, to say yes to this time of fertility. Create a sumptuously beautiful home or garden full of rich colors, or a table set for a feast of delectable dishes made with aromatic spices. Or simply create artistically. And take time to savor! It's important to take pleasure in what you've created.

Decoding the Symbolism

The Empress is card number three, and three has an energy we all like. It's marked by beauty, sharing, connection, expression, and the richness of creating and enjoying life. This card is usually full of inviting colors: yellows, pinks, oranges, and greens. Most decks portray The Empress herself as a full-figured woman, sitting regally yet comfortably in a cushy chair. She is often surrounded by wheat, fruits, and flowering trees, which indicate the abundance Mother Earth has to offer. Along with features that are warm and pleasing, The Empress wears a crown that signifies she's self-realized. She has said "yes!" to herself and is relishing her manifestations. And she calls you to do the same for yourself.

IV · The Emperor

THE EMPEROR

The Emperor is a commanding force. He is his own authority, and he's not afraid to use his power to move forward in the world. But there's nothing reckless about this energy. The Emperor is like Captain Kirk from *Star Trek*, knowing he has command of the ship and it's time to boldly go where no man has gone before.

The Emperor possesses a capable, pioneering energy, very masculine and strong. His courageous nature is at its best when fully engaged in meaningful pursuit of his endeavors. This archetype needs a cause or a meaty project on which to focus his tremendous energy. Otherwise, The Emperor can become tyrannical.

If this card shows up in a reading, it's time to take initiative on your own projects. You are the king of your own domain. You have the tools and knowledge to take action. Don't be afraid to lead, even if you're just leading yourself. Tap into The Emperor's strength and take charge!

Decoding the Symbolism

You'll usually find The Emperor sitting on a throne, indicating that he (like The Empress) knows his place and is in charge of his surroundings. He also wears a crown and holds a staff, signifying that he is self-realized and has the tools to lead. (Think Moses banging his staff on the ground to part the Red Sea and lead the Israelites to freedom.)

Associated with the number four and the earth element, The Emperor is also grounded, pragmatic, and all about worldly affairs. You may see him in a red robe—a color of passion and spiritual authority—but The Emperor isn't a hothead. He observes the world around him from an elevated seat, so he knows the time is right to move forward. This card is calling you to trust yourself and your experience, and to move ahead with confidence.

V · The Hierophant

This is a card of spiritual authority. The Hierophant is, in many ways, a high priest. He's the one The Empress and Emperor go to for spiritual guidance. He's also ordained and has the responsibility of conducting rites, which is why he's often associated with marriage. If you're seeing this card in a reading, it may be telling you to keep an eye out for a spiritual teacher. In fact, it often indicates that one is on their way to you already.

THE HIEROPHANT

Traditionally, spiritual wisdom has been the domain of formal religions. But today, we know that spiritual teachers can come from anywhere—and you never even have to meet them in person! You might find yours in a book recommended by a friend, or a podcast recommended by an algorithm. You may even look to your own ancestry. Whether you find your "aha" moments in Paramahansa Yogananda or Eckhart Tolle, choose a teacher you feel drawn to. The point is that there's valuable spiritual guidance available to you right now if you're open to finding it.

Decoding the Symbolism

As card number five, The Hierophant signifies a changing point. Five seeks new stimuli in the world around it, and The Hierophant is a card of new ideas and information—in this case, *spiritual* information. You'll often see him dressed in red, a color of spiritual authority. Classically, The Hierophant has been portrayed as the Pope or a sanctioned leader of a religious organization. And Catholics may recognize the card's main motifs, such as Peter being granted the keys to the kingdom. The imagery in most modern decks, however, represents a more universal spiritual teacher who can hail from any faith (or no faith). But in all versions, The Hierophant is the intermediary between the Divine and worldly, and he's calling you to seek out spiritual wisdom because you're ready to learn and grow in your spirituality.

VI · The Lovers

All you romantics out there will probably be happy to see this card pop up in your reading. Yes, pulling The Lovers signifies that attraction, romance, and sex are in the cards for you (literally). But it's not necessarily all about passion. This card indicates that, at this time, your growth depends on relating to another person.

The Lovers card is about the union of opposites. This card brings together the masculine and feminine archetypes of the preceding cards—The Emperor and The Empress. Now they've been sanctioned by the priest (The Hierophant) and are joined to further their evolution.

This card points to different experiences depending on your situation. If you're single, someone who will really turn your head may be coming into your life. For those already in a relationship, this card could indicate that you need to put more time and energy into your partnership. (Think date night with your spouse.) But in relation to the surrounding cards in the spread, The Lovers could have deeper implications about needing to look at the quality of your relationship and ask some meaningful questions about it.

Decoding the Symbolism

The Lovers is card number six, and the energy of six is all about love, home, family, and the personal sphere. Many decks show a couple facing each other, illustrating the theme of needing to relate to one another. Often, they stand before an angel, signifying spiritual forces bringing them together. Sometimes, it's a capricious cupid above them—a symbol of Eros and romantic love.

In the Rider-Waite deck, the couple are naked, and there's a serpent wrapped around a tree behind the woman, referencing Adam and Eve before the fall. So you can expect an element of chaos on the relationship front with this card. But isn't that always the case when falling in love?

VII · The Chariot

The Chariot represents a vehicle—in modern times, a car. But this vehicle symbolizes more than transportation. In dreams, a car represents how you move through the world. The model, color, and condition of your car in a dream will say a lot about your state of mind. The energy of this card is about planning and preparing, getting a clear idea of where you want to go (in travel or in life).

Imagine you're going on a road trip from New York to Los Angeles. You wouldn't just hop in the car and go. You might get your car serviced. You would decide what you are going to bring with you and pack accordingly. And you would map out a basic route with stops along the way. That's the kind of planning this card calls for.

This card in a reading indicates you are getting ready for a journey and need to think things through. There's a degree of introspection required here. What are you good at? Where do you want to be? The Chariot calls for a meditative approach to life and advises you not to go off half-cocked; instead, take the time to plan and prepare once you are clear in yourself.

Decoding the Symbolism

The imagery of this card is almost always of a man in an old-fashioned chariot. He is often dressed as a knight, so he has some status and independence. The man stands in the cart, looking out to the future. Although the man in The Chariot hasn't started moving yet, he's set his sights on his destination. This man knows he is about to start the next leg of his journey and will be ready to cover new terrain. Combine that message with the numerology: "Know thyself" is seven's mantra—it's the number of introspection. It represents the mind, somewhat objective and analytical. With clarity, you're ready for any adventure!

VIII · Strength

Courage and confidence

The Strength card calls you to tap into your inner power. It signifies the fire of the solar plexus chakra, the energy center located between your rib cage and belly button. This area is called the solar plexus because it radiates like the sun.

Put your hand on your solar plexus and take a few deep breaths. Feel that inner sun and let it radiate out, because you have the power within you. Sometimes we forget that, so this card is an encouraging reminder. It tells you that, no matter what's going on in your life, *you've got this!* Strength is about having the courage to stand by your convictions, and relying on your willpower and fortitude to see you through. Trust yourself and the energy that's guiding you.

Decoding the Symbolism

Power, energy, and ambition are all hallmarks of the number eight. Like the sun, this number is a self-sustaining force. On its side, it's the symbol for infinity. And that's how it shows up in the Rider-Waite deck, hovering over the head of a woman to signify that she's tapped into that unending energy. She is also standing with a male lion, often seen subduing him without force by holding his jaws, although some decks portray the woman and the lion peacefully coexisting. The lion represents powerful instincts. This animal is at the top of the food chain but only hunts and eats what he needs to survive. He's both powerful and in control of himself. This imagery is a call to tap into your primal energies, trusting that you have the awareness to use your power appropriately.

IX · The Hermit

The spiritual adept

The Hermit takes the path less traveled. He is autonomous. He follows his own way, guided by his spiritual practice and the lantern he carries. These light the way for him, so he doesn't need anything outside of himself to see his path.

This card is about stepping off the busy, paved road to follow the rough path that cuts through the woods. People don't always like seeing The Hermit in a reading because it's a call to separate from the collective and find your own way. But if this card shows up for you, it's because you are capable of doing just that.

Autonomy is a good thing. It doesn't mean you have to be alone; it means you aren't afraid to be alone. Once you embrace the energy of The Hermit, it produces a sense of peace, calm, and spaciousness. This card signals you to put your spiritual beliefs into practice—to walk the walk and really follow the best path for *you*. The light of your spirituality is with you, guiding you and allowing you to go your own way.

Decoding the Symbolism

Nine is the last number in numerology. It represents maturity, wisdom, and reaching the peak. Accordingly, The Hermit is shown as a cloaked wise man carrying a lantern and a walking stick. In most decks, he looks like Gandalf from *The Lord of the Rings*. He is serene and self-contained. The Hermit is often seen walking into the mountains, which represent the elevated consciousness of the spiritual adept (spiritual master). He isn't antisocial (Gandalf was always hanging out with the Hobbits); he's simply living on another plane of consciousness. And he is quiet about it. The Hermit tells you that you have a great opportunity to step off the noisy, well-trodden path and follow your light. Just as he has his walking stick—his tool to navigate rough terrain—you have everything you need to get to the top of the mountain.

X • The Wheel of Fortune

Fortuitous change

WHEEL OF FORTUNE

Your world is spinning faster! Chance encounters, new opportunities, and expansion are the domain of The Wheel of Fortune. This card signifies that positive prospects surround you or will soon be coming. The Wheel of Fortune builds on The Chariot, Strength, and The Hermit before it. With preparation (The Chariot), increased confidence in your own power (Strength), and the willingness to follow an unmarked path (The Hermit), your outer world begins to shift around you. And its pace is picking up!

If you've been yearning to be more successful, to move to a new location, or to simply have more action in your life, know that it's coming. This card has fortune in its name, so it's also a good indicator on the money front. As a sign of major positive change in your world, The Wheel of Fortune suggests it's a good time to make big moves— put your house up for sale, expand your business, pop the question. You can expect greater excitement and energy in the happenings around you.

Decoding the Symbolism

Lucky number ten gives this card a positive spin. One represents you, and zero represents the Divine, meaning you're in a good place when this card shows up. Wheels, of course, indicate movement. But the Wheel also represents both the Milky Way galaxy and the fixed constellations of the zodiac. The Earth—our perspective—is the hub, and the constellations are the spokes circling around and around.

The esoteric symbolism here refers to how we move through the wheel of time. The seasons are always changing—nothing is static. However, we do have fixed points of reference to understand where we are at any given time. The Wheel of Fortune reflects this and, if it appears in your reading, indicates that this is a season of expansion and opportunity for you. So don't let it pass you by!

XI · Justice

Balance and clear thinking

They say "justice is blind"—it asks us to be truly impartial, not looking at appearances but instead going deeper and listening to all the evidence. And that's the intention of this card. Tarot's Justice signifies weighing things mindfully and arriving at a clear decision. The energy of this card also speaks to taking the middle road, not leaning toward any extreme. This is where the answers lie, and we avoid swinging the pendulum in either direction with our bias. The result is a verdict that's clear and unbiased.

Just as a judge listens to both sides and considers all evidence before arriving at a verdict, Justice calls you to do the same. This card focuses on the mental realm. Step back from emotion and reactivity—in other words, *detach*. Then you will gain clarity and insight into whatever situation you're facing. This could be between you and another person, or between two aspects of a problem you're seeking answers to. From a place of balance, you can see a solution.

Decoding the Symbolism

As card number eleven (a powerful Master Number), Justice evokes the number two (one plus one), which is about balance and diplomacy, compromise and listening. Eleven is calling the energy of number two to a higher order. Justice represents the highest court. She usually sits between two pillars on a raised platform, signifying that her consciousness is higher and removed from those around her.

Justice often holds a scale in her left hand and an upright sword in her right hand—left represents the past, right the future. The scales represent balance. Justice calls forth careful consideration and asks you to seek a win-win solution. The upright sword, which symbolizes the air element in Tarot, points to a clear idea. After weighing the evidence, you have the power to make a clear, informed decision.

XII · The Hanged Man

Total surrender

THE HANGED MAN

If The Hanged Man appears in your reading, it's time to let it go. There's nothing else you can do in this situation. We don't usually like to hear this message, but it can be such a relief. Whatever your circumstances, you've done all you can. Now it's time to hand the outcome over to the Universe.

If you trust that the Universe has your back, no matter what, then you'll be able to relax when you see this card. But if you have a more fearful view of a higher power, then surrendering will feel scary. So there's a deeper meaning to The Hanged Man about exploring your relationship with the Divine. The good news is that this is ultimately a card of grace. You have a window of opportunity to release your attachment to an outcome that you may be desperately holding on to. If you let go, then you leave space for magic and favor, and circumstances can shift in a way that benefits all.

Decoding the Symbolism

The number twelve indicates letting go of your ego. The number one represents your sense of self, and two represents your heart. Added together, they make three and create something more: the ability to release limiting beliefs and let your heart guide you.

The Hanged Man is portrayed as a man hanging upside down from his foot—not his neck! He's not in danger. Instead, he represents a 180-degree shift in perspective. It feels counterintuitive because the ego wants to hold on no matter what. But when we let go of our position, we can see everything in a new light. That's the meaning of the halo or golden light often seen surrounding his head—illumination! This is a profound symbol of the possibilities you can awaken by surrendering. A higher power is offering you a solution; you just need to let go and allow it.

XIII • Death

Death usually provokes the most fear, but remember: Tarot is a book of symbolism. This card indicates that you are transforming on a profound level. It represents an organic process in which a natural ending allows for a new beginning. And while you don't know what will happen next, you have an opportunity to meet the unknown with bravery and trust.

Another way to understand Death is to look at the transformation of a caterpillar into a butterfly. Once the caterpillar is ready to undergo the next stage in its development, it makes a cocoon, it disintegrates, and it begins to reconstitute itself into a new form: a butterfly. Then the cocoon falls away, and the butterfly spreads its wings. It's not just free—it can fly! It's no longer confined to inching slowly across the surface of its environment. So ask yourself: would you rather be a caterpillar or a butterfly? The metamorphic process of Death is what allows for this transformation.

Decoding the Symbolism

Thirteen is, appropriately, the number of transformation. In numerology, thirteen is equal to the number four (one plus three). Four is about security, hanging onto the status quo. The one and three of thirteen represent a new process of creative change. So transformation of established structures or ideas is the name of this card's game. The classic symbolism of this card is the ol' Grim Reaper riding in on his white horse. But the horse represents graceful movement, and white is the color of purity. This transformation is a natural, organic process.

Death also carries a scythe, a tool for harvesting crops. How can wheat be made into flour for bread if it's still growing in the field? The crop has to be cut and harvested. And bread is life. The death of one form allows for a new process that will feed and nourish you.

XIV · Temperance

Integration and wholeness

After the intensity of Death, Temperance offers a time of reintegration and equilibrium. This card signifies the alchemy inherent in blending masculine and feminine energies. The dance of these opposites brings wholeness. Think of it like the yin-yang symbol of traditional Chinese philosophy. The black of yin contains a dot of yang's white, and the white of yang carries a dot of yin's black. They are fluid, balanced, swirling together, and transcending duality as polar opposites that create a unified whole.

Temperance indicates that you have the consciousness to see this integration in yourself now. This is a card of deep psychological awareness (so it might signal that it's a good time for psychotherapy or Jungian dream work). The integration of the shadow into light enhances your understanding of your true nature. This card points to the sacred marriage of what Jung describes as the anima and animus—our internal feminine and masculine sides. While The Lovers is a card about our relationship to another, Temperance is about having a harmonious relationship with the different aspects of *yourself*.

Decoding the Symbolism

The number fourteen indicates grounded change: something new (one) in your structure (four) allows for new activity or communication (five). In classic Tarot, the Temperance card features an androgynous figure pouring water between two cups. Water represents emotions and an awareness of your feelings. The suit of Cups also represents this in Tarot. Sometimes the figure is portrayed with one foot in water and one foot on land, blending the elements of water and earth and indicating a grounded understanding that you can feel in your body. In the Rider-Waite deck, there's a path leading into the mountains, over which hangs a crown of illumination. All of this is to say that you're on the path to greater consciousness and self-realization.

XV · The Devil

The Devil is the most misunderstood card in Tarot. And understandably so! It evokes fear and superstition. But you may be surprised by its true meaning. Satan in Hebrew means "the adversary." This is the force that's always testing us, pulling us away from Source and into chaos, and leading us from a spiritual perspective of abundance into the lack mentality of materialism.

This card represents the confines of social conditioning and beliefs that contribute to scarcity, poverty, and lack of love. The Devil is saying, "Don't believe everything the world has taught you!" Recognize how you've been shaped and molded by the opinions of others and how these limiting beliefs are shackling you. It's time to free yourself from these beliefs, to draw on your innate light, and to boldly move forward. Depending on the surrounding cards, this card can indicate negativity around you. People may mean well, but be careful not to buy into their fearful ideas. Think for yourself and trust your instincts.

Decoding the Symbolism

Fifteen is a number of emancipation. The individuality of one works with the active energy of five to free you from a situation involving six (home, family, and relationships). This card's number points to releasing yourself from some of the beliefs that may have been instilled in you growing up, but that are now impeding your actualization, happiness, and freedom to be your authentic self.

The classic versions of this card show The Lovers, chains around their necks, with the Devil looming over them. This points to a couple being caught in societal roles that are restricting them. But upon closer inspection, you see that the chains are loose—they can liberate themselves by letting go of the superstition that doing so is wrong. This is a card of empowerment, telling you to wake up and be free.

XVI · The Tower

Destruction of the old paradigm

At its essence, The Tower is a healing crisis. This is not a subtle energy. A construct that you've been living in is falling apart. This can produce some anxious feelings—the mind wants stability and continuity even if that stability isn't in your best interest. The best way to meet this energy is to trust that the Universe knows what's right for you. Let the old system collapse; it no longer serves you.

When this card is in a reading, it's guiding you to trust the storm. Though it's loud, the thunder and lightning are scary, and gale-force winds are shaking the very structure that you call home, the storm is necessary. And it won't kill you! After the storm passes and the debris settles, you'll emerge feeling lighter. The Tower is telling you that you've outgrown the situation you've been living in, whether a job, a relationship, or a deeply held belief system. At one time, this structure served you and sheltered you, but, at some point, it became a prison. The storm has come to free you.

Decoding the Symbolism

The Tower is number sixteen, which reduces to seven (one plus six) and indicates your consciousness and the way you think. The number one represents your identity, and six represents your home, family, and relationships. So sixteen signifies a breakthrough in consciousness, an opportunity to release limiting beliefs about yourself and your life.

In most decks, you'll see a medieval tower being struck by lightning. It's on fire, and a man and woman are falling through the air. The tower image represents a major construct in your life. Fire is a purifying element, burning the old to make way for the new. The man and woman are pushed out of the tower, signaling the necessary end of the paradigm they've been living in. Although it comes with an alarming image, this shakeup will be to your benefit.

XVII • The Star

After The Tower's storm clouds have moved out, the sky is clear. You can now find your way by following the light of your guiding star. Think of the wise men following the star of the East, or the ancient Polynesians using celestial navigation to find the tiny archipelago of Hawaii in thousands of miles of open ocean. That is The Star: a crystallized vision and guiding light by which you can navigate.

This card signals a time when you will have a vision for your life, one that you can trust will guide you. This energy is lofty. A higher vision is leading you to greater clarity around your purpose—what you are meant to do, be, and accomplish in this life. Once you've identified your guiding star, it will always be there; you'll know where in the vast sky to look. The Star will bring you to the fullest expression of your talents.

Decoding the Symbolism

As card number seventeen, The Star heralds a new vision and clarity of mind. One and seven added together make the number eight, signifying your true ambition and the successful fulfillment of this vision. Eight has to do with what you wish to accomplish in the world. And the numbers one and seven indicate that this comes from deep inside you.

Most decks show a woman pouring water onto the earth with stars above her, shining down their radiant light. This indicates brilliant thinking that is also emotionally nourishing. She is following her highest guiding principle and, in doing so, is filled emotionally. She then pours that fulfillment back into her surroundings. This is a beautiful process. When you follow your guiding star, you fill your cup and can then share that bounty with others.

XVIII • The Moon

The Moon is tricky, with a deceptive quality to its light. In many ways, this card is a "heads up." Have you noticed that, not long after you've made a big decision, you find yourself facing a challenge? Your instinctual response is to go back the way you came. The Moon is a call to *not* do that. It's saying that, although it feels more comfortable to do what you've always done, you would be simply repeating an old pattern. There is a saying that the definition of insanity (aka lunacy) is doing the same thing over and over again and hoping for a different result.

When this card appears in a reading, expect that fears will arise, but know that fear is not a signal to stop or go back. Instead, it indicates that you're at the threshold of something new and potentially amazing. Keep moving forward. Feel the fear and do it anyway!

Decoding the Symbolism

Eighteen is a sacred number. In Kabbalah, it is called *chai*, the Hebrew word for *life*. The number one represents a new beginning, and eight represents the strength of your desires. When added, they produce nine, which signifies reaching the pinnacle. This combination indicates new birth after a full gestation.

This card often shows the moon illuminating a path at night. Symbolically, the moon represents your emotional body, your unconscious instinctual self. The path goes from the water of your emotions to the mountains of higher consciousness. In the Rider-Waite deck, on the left side of the path is a wolf (primal instincts) and on the right is a dog (trustworthy companion). The left is the past and the right is the future. You need to choose: Do you follow the path you've been on, which will only lead to more of the same? Or do you trust the future with all its possibilities? Turn right and keep your eyes on the path. It will be dawn soon, and you'll see that you made the right choice.

XIX · The Sun

Happiness and fulfillment

This is the card of happier times—a new day and a new dawn. It heralds fulfillment and joy. In a relationship, it indicates that the right partners have found each other. There is a childlike quality to this card—it calls you to play, enjoy, and be unceasingly optimistic. Look at everything with new eyes! After the long, strange night of The Moon, The Sun has risen. And it brings excitement and brightens the terrain around you. The birds are chirping, the dew on the grass is sparkling, and you can feel the warmth of the sun's rays on your skin.

The energy of this card is like having driven all night to get to your vacation spot. You may have gotten lost along the way or wondered whether the little beach house you rented online is going to be a dump. But as you pull into the driveway, the sun is rising, and everything looks perfect. When The Sun appears in your reading, brighter days are ahead.

Decoding the Symbolism

Nineteen is a very optimistic number combination indeed! The newness of the number one finds its exaltation in the nine to produce ten: luck and opportunity that promises a new beginning. Symbolically, The Sun represents life-giving light, just like the sun in the sky. Yellow is a color of joy and life force. The solar plexus chakra (which is also yellow) is the energy center of your body.

This card is typically illustrated with bright colors, flowers, and a clear blue sky. In the classic decks, two children are playing happily. In the Rider-Waite deck, a smiling child rides a white horse. Children represent innocence, looking at the world through fresh eyes, while the white horse represents purity and graceful movement. The iconography of The Sun always exemplifies fun and happiness. School's out, and it's summertime at last!

XX · Judgment

Full awareness

The Judgment card tells us the veil has lifted. This card is associated with Judgment Day—as in, the Apocalypse. But before you get nervous, realize that *apocalypse* is a Greek word meaning *to reveal*. This card is not about the end of the world; it's about having a revelation. It signifies being able to see the big picture and having great awareness and objectivity about yourself or the situation around you. This card brings good news, and what was hidden becomes obvious.

Tarot's Judgment also doesn't signify judgment in a negative way—as in being judged or being judgmental. When this card comes up in a reading (depending on the placement in a spread), it says clarity is coming. The aperture on the camera lens will go from telephoto to wide angle so you can see the whole landscape. Maybe you didn't have all the facts before, but soon you will. What seemed concealed will be revealed. And that will produce some "aha" moments for you!

Decoding the Symbolism

The number twenty combines the intuition, balance, and feeling of two with the grace of zero. This is an opening to understand yourself or your relationship with another in a greater light. Judgment signifies a new era, one of peace and unity. The symbolism of this card in classical Tarot is very biblical. It references Judgment Day, when the dead rise. You see archangel Gabriel blowing his horn, calling for goodness to prevail, and people rising from their coffins to celebrate. At its core, this is a powerful motif of resurrection and a clear message that what is truly for you won't pass you. What was buried will be unearthed, and a new era will begin. The essence of what you want may seem long gone, but it is about to be brought to life again in a new light.

XXI · The World

The journey that began with The Fool reaches its culmination with The World. Things have come full circle, yes, but on a higher plane. The Fool is about trust and blind faith in the Divine. The World signals that you are fully conscious of being one with the Divine. (Kind of a big deal!)

Think of seeing The World as putting the last piece in place on a big jigsaw puzzle that you've been working on. You knew what the puzzle looked like; you picked it out because of the pretty picture on the box. But dumping the pieces on the table began a process. And in the meditation of slowly building the image, you saw different aspects of it. Your consciousness evolved. As you finish it, you feel the satisfaction of having fully participated in its creation. This card encourages you to savor this moment in your life—to look around you and recognize what you've done, and to see yourself as a builder of worlds.

Decoding the Symbolism

Number twenty-one is a number of harmony, balance, and completion. The combination of two and one, three, represents beauty and aesthetics. The vibration of this number combination is one of divine proportion experienced in the material world.

The classical versions of this card portray a woman floating in the sky, surrounded by a large laurel wreath, which is a symbol of triumph. The wreath forms a circle— the geometry of the Divine, the Alpha and the Omega. The woman holds a baton in each hand, signaling balance between the masculine and feminine polarities, and the completion of the manifestation begun with The Magician (who holds one baton).

This is some heady symbolism! It signifies achievement, wholeness, and oneness with the Universe. It also indicates a favorable completion of a journey—be it physical, emotional, or spiritual—that has touched all the elements in your life. Enjoy this time of triumph, because a new journey is about to begin!

Ace of Wands

A bold new start

Ace (new beginnings) + Wands (fire and action) = bold energy

The Ace of Wands is a big-energy card—your inner fire is lit, and you can tap into this potent energy to boldly go forth. This is the time for inspired new action. You're being given an opening to move forward; feel your power and use it to initiate something new in your life.

ACE OF WANDS

Two of Wands

Weighing the possibilities

Two (balance) + Wands (fire and action) = possible actions

The Two of Wands tells you that you have at least a couple options available to you right now. This is a positive card and a good position to be in. You have the freedom of deciding for yourself how you want to move forward. Enjoy the spaciousness of having choices.

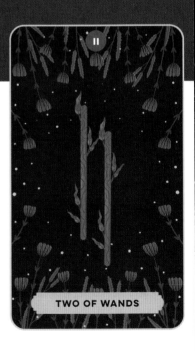

TWO OF WANDS

Three of Wands

Three (harmonics) + Wands (fire and action) = alignment

You stand perched on fertile ground, with several projects poised to move forward. The energy of the Three of Wands comes not from a place of stress, but from a place of order. The different aspects of your life are in sync. Your personal, professional, and spiritual life are in harmony and will play out accordingly.

THREE OF WANDS

Four of Wands

Joyful participation

Four (stability) + Wands (fire and action) = active collaboration to manifest

The Four of Wands is a wonderfully positive signifier. You have the opportunity to work with others now, and there's a good exchange of give-and-take available between you. What you build together will work out.

FOUR OF WANDS

Five of Wands

Five (changeability) + Wands (fire and action) = confusion

The Five of Wands indicates scattered energy. You're trying to make things happen and may feel overwhelmed or conflicted. This card's advice is to take it easy. Just do what you have to do and no more. There's change in the air, so less is more right now.

FIVE OF WANDS

Six of Wands

Success

Six (personal responsibility) + Wands (fire and action) = achievement

The Six of Wands is a card of victory. Something has worked out, or will soon work out, in your life. You'll know when it happens because you'll feel the energetic lift that accompanies success and satisfaction. Enjoy this time of achievement.

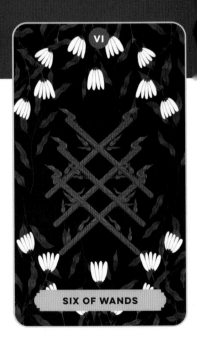

SIX OF WANDS

Seven of Wands

Standing your ground

Seven (introspection) + Wands (fire and action) = wise actions

The Seven of Wands asks you to consider how you're expending your energy. Are you so distracted by the needs of others that you're losing yourself in the process? Think of the safety demo on an airplane: put on your own oxygen mask first so you can help those around you. Your compassion toward others is commendable, but heed this card's reminder to take care of yourself as well.

Eight of Wands

Swift movement

Eight (power) + Wands (fire and action) = velocity

The Eight of Wands is the travel card. This is a time of movement and of swift progress toward your destination. This might refer to a place you want to travel to, or it might refer to a goal you've set for yourself. The wind is at your back, and you can now fly with ease.

Nine of Wands

NINE OF WANDS

Nine (culmination) + Wands (fire and action) = maximum output

The Nine of Wands acknowledges that you've been working long, hard hours. Life has been demanding, and you've been handling it all but are getting tired. There are times in life when things are full tilt, and this is one of them. This isn't a negative card; it's simply a reminder to recognize the need to replenish your energy.

Ten of Wands

Carrying a load

TEN OF WANDS

Ten (endings and new beginnings) + Wands (fire and action) = breakthroughs and release

The Ten of Wands signifies a heavy load. You're strong—you can handle a lot. You keep moving forward, but what should have been just a sprint has turned into a marathon. Being overloaded has become the norm. You're due for a break-through. Don't worry—you will cross the finish line!

Page of Wands

The Page of Wands represents the childlike quality of fire—bubbling energy, playfulness, and zeal. This card is telling you to lighten up! Put on some music and dance around your living room. Go to the beach and play in the waves. There's a call to both fearlessness and innocence here. Stop worrying about all that so-called adult stuff and trust that everything in your world is going to work out.

Page of Wands as a Person

PAGE OF WANDS

This card can also represent a child or very youthful person who is entering your life or is already in your life (or an aspect of yourself). The Page of Wands is the youth of the fire signs, signifying children or teenagers with their sun or rising sign in Aries, Leo, or Sagittarius. This person's childlike enthusiasm is infectious—they're here to get you to drop your responsibilities, go out, and have some fun. When was the last time you went to a concert or an amusement park? Enjoy yourself!

Knight of Wands

KNIGHT OF WANDS

Knights always signify movement (that's why they're often portrayed riding a horse). This knight carries a wand, symbolizing the element of fire, so this card's energy needs to move fast. The Knight of Wands is actively engaged in the pursuit of goals. It calls you to not just get moving, but to follow your passion with laser focus. Don't do the boring stuff; do what lights you up. Be driven, ambitious, and intense. You can make great strides right now and cover a lot of ground quickly. If you've felt low lately, this energy will light a fire under you and get you motivated.

Knight of Wands as a Person

This card can also indicate that a very fiery young adult is in your life or is coming soon. The Knight of Wands represents someone in their twenties with their sun or rising sign in Aries, Leo, or Sagittarius who likes to be physically active. They bring with them a lot of crackling energy. This person is the type to move fast, to get up early to go jogging, and to talk you into going on a road trip with them. They're here to wake you up and to help you realize that there are so many interesting things to see and do. Get moving!

Queen of Wands

Queens represent the feminine nature of an element—in this case, fire. The feminine aspects of a person are their caring, loving, nurturing qualities. Fire is warm and lively, expressive and demonstrative. With all of these traits coming together in the Queen of Wands, this card tells you that you have an abundance of positive energy to share. In your work, this card might mean showing up to help your colleagues or going the extra mile in a project. On the personal front, this card tells you it's a good time to ask someone to dinner or throw a party. You have talents and gifts to share, and, when you do, it will give you even more energy.

QUEEN OF WANDS

Queen of Wands as a Person

This card can also signal that a warm and giving person (usually a woman) is in or coming into your life. They radiate the boundless energy of Aries, the sweetness of Leo, or the adventurousness of Sagittarius. This might be an old friend who reaches out and invites you to spend time together, or a sister coming to visit who helps bring warmth and energy into your life. It could also represent you. This person's energy indicates that this is a time to be nurturing and share yourself.

King of Wands

KING OF WANDS

Kings are the masculine aspect of a suit and the full maturation of their element. The King of Wands (fire) represents the qualities of leadership and inspired action, strength and control. This card signals you to use your power, considerable knowledge, and energy for the highest good. Harness your creativity and manifest your desires. Take charge in your work or relationship. Delegate and direct others so joint projects work out successfully and efficiently. There is a need for your expertise, and sharing your gifts will benefit everyone around you.

King of Wands as a Person

This card can also signal that a dynamic, accomplished person (often a man) with their sun or rising sign in Aries, Leo, or Sagittarius is coming into your life. They have a lot of charisma, are a force of positivity and optimism, and have a natural take-charge attitude. This person's vision and ability to walk the walk can inspire you to action. They can teach you how to harness your own energy and move confidently in the direction of your dreams. The King of Wands leads you by example!

Ace of Pentacles

ACE OF PENTACLES

Receiving an offering

Ace (new beginnings) + Pentacles (earth and the material) = a gift

The Ace of Pentacles represents being offered something material. A new job might open up that has all the potential to take your career where you want it to go. Or seed money for your next venture might come to you from an unexpected source. This card carries the energy of a concrete opportunity. Take it!

Two of Pentacles

TWO OF PENTACLES

Step by step

Two (balance) + Pentacles (earth and the material) = holding pattern

The Two of Pentacles calls you to do just what is right in front of you. Keep your eyes on the path at your feet and follow the breadcrumbs one by one. It's also OK to wait and see. It can actually be restful. This can feel like a time of limbo, but there's nothing more you can do right now. It will become clear when it's time to make bigger moves.

Three of Pentacles

Gradual progress

Three (harmonics) + Pentacles (earth and the material) = steady work

The energy of the Three of Pentacles is that of measured forward movement. Nothing about the earth element is fast. (Speed is the domain of the Wands and fire.) But this element is grounded. This card signals that, if you keep moving slowly and steadily, you will get to your desired destination.

THREE OF PENTACLES

Four of Pentacles

Rigidity

Four (stability) + Pentacles (earth and the material) = contraction

The Four of Pentacles is basically earth plus earth, so its energy is heavy. When this card comes up, it's telling you that you're holding on too tightly to something. It might be your money or your energy. Or maybe your schedule is too rigid and fixed. You're limiting your perspective by placing too much consideration on the material aspects of your life. Loosen up!

FOUR OF PENTACLES

Five of Pentacles

FIVE OF PENTACLES

Five (changeability) + Pentacles (earth and the material) = survival fears

No matter which deck you use, the Five of Pentacles is dismal looking. This card represents fear and worry that you won't have enough resources. This is a call to take a deep breath—do not fall prey to pessimism. Even if your situation feels dire in this moment, stay calm and take a step back, and you will see a way forward.

Six of Pentacles

SIX OF PENTACLES

Security

Six (personal responsibility) + Pentacles (earth and the material) = playing things safe

How you experience the Six of Pentacles can depend on your current definition of security. This card carries the energy of doing the safe, familiar thing and succeeding at it. But staying in your comfort zone doesn't allow for a lot of growth or upward mobility. This card calls you to expect more and consider what would bring more fulfillment in your present situation.

Seven of Pentacles

Patience required

SEVEN OF PENTACLES

Seven (introspection) + Pentacles (earth and the material) = gestation time

The Seven of Pentacles reminds you that seeds need time and nurturing to grow. This card calls for patience with and understanding of some process in your life. Maybe you started something new a couple of months ago and thought you'd see results by now. You might start to question yourself and your efforts—pessimism is a default position when things don't go according to our timing. But there's no reason to despair. Instead, stay the course and expect good things.

Eight of Pentacles

Growth and persistence

EIGHT OF PENTACLES

Eight (power) + Pentacles (earth and the material) = outer development

The Eight of Pentacles tells you that you're gaining ground in an endeavor. This card carries the energy of springtime, not summer—the buds are just beginning to open but aren't yet flowering. But you can still go outside without a coat, breathe in the fresh air, and smile at the bulbs that have risen up through the soil. In other words, enjoy the process. Whatever you hope to manifest is already on its way.

Nine of Pentacles

NINE OF PENTACLES

Nine (culmination) + Pentacles (earth and the material) = fruition

The Nine of Pentacles carries the energy of a situation fully maturing. This card is good news for projects coming to completion after a lot of work. It might also indicate a situation in your personal life that you've been patiently putting energy into finally shifting in a positive direction. It can signify material growth and fruition as well, making it a good indicator for money or investments.

Ten of Pentacles

TEN OF PENTACLES

Inner and outer wealth

Ten (endings and new beginnings) + Pentacles (earth and the material) = abundance

The Ten of Pentacles is a great signifier for positive developments in your life. It indicates that you've grown in your own capacities, and your material life shows it. This is the classic card of wealth and sharing wealth. Your network or community is increasing and bringing a rich exchange on many levels. Look for ways to keep expanding your circle or engaging more fully with the people around you.

Page of Pentacles

PAGE OF PENTACLES

The Page of Pentacles is the student, taking classes in numerous subjects, all relating to how things work on the material plane. They're diligently learning and developing the skills to navigate this world. Is there a new subject you want to learn? Are you contemplating a new hobby or increasing your skill set? This card signals that it's a good time to get going on that pursuit or at least do some research so you can start the process.

Page of Pentacles as a Person

The Page of Pentacles can also represent a young person with their sun or rising sign in Taurus, Virgo, or Capricorn who is in your life or on their way to you. Theirs is an energy of someone who is eager to learn. This person may be starting an adventure or just beginning to build something. And this person could be you! Think of a child with a block of dough, moving it through their hands to soften it and start to sculpt something. This card's message encourages you to approach new endeavors with an open mind.

Knight of Pentacles

Knights are always on the move. The energy of the Knight of Pentacles exemplifies testing out your skills. Think apprentice—you've already gone through the book-learning phase and are now learning by doing. The pace here is steady. Measured movement is the best way to further your interests. Take the time to refine your skills.

Knight of Pentacles as a Person

Depending on its placement and the other cards in a spread, the Knight of Pentacles can also indicate a strong young adult whose sun or rising sign is in Virgo, Capricorn, or Taurus. This person's energy is practical and thoughtful. They are moving toward their goals, steadily making progress, and they have the endurance to keep going.

And, of course, this may be referring to you or an aspect of yourself—in which case, slow and steady wins the race.

Queen of Pentacles

Beauty and fertility

QUEEN OF PENTACLES

As the feminine aspect of earth, the Queen of Pentacles represents caring for the body and health. This card indicates that this is a good time to take care of yourself—eat nutritious food that fuels you, buy clothes that make you feel good, or just take some me-time. It's OK to spend a little money. The Queen of Pentacles reminds you that self-care is not a luxury; it is essential for your well-being. She can also signify motherhood because she is fertile and pregnant with possibilities ready to manifest beautifully into the world.

Queen of Pentacles as a Person

The Queen of Pentacles is the minor arcana's version of The Empress, and creativity, abundance, beautiful flowers, good food, and fine clothes are her milieu. This card can represent someone (usually a woman) whose sun or rising sign is in Taurus, Virgo, or Capricorn. This person takes care of themself, appreciates beauty, loves the finer things, and surrounds themself with material abundance. They're always sprucing up their home and garden, spending time on improving the aesthetics around them. If someone comes into your life with these qualities, this card may be reminding you to take care of yourself and appreciate the beauty around you too.

King of Pentacles

The King of Pentacles is the masculine aspect of the earth element, using his skills to provide material security and abundance. He is the successful businessman, the good investor—a man of maturity and stature. He has good timing, doesn't rush, and knows when to make something happen and when to sit back and let it all come together. The King of Pentacles is also endowed with manifesting skills, making him a great indicator of money to come. This card's energy brings material security.

KING OF PENTACLES

King of Pentacles as a Person

The king of the earth element is the master of the material world. His natural inclination is toward work and enjoying the fruits of his labor. If you are a woman and this card comes up in your reading, it can represent the soulmate within. You have access to the full support of your own male energy—the part of you that creates stability and material well-being. The King of Pentacles can also indicate that you've met or will soon meet an important man, possibly with his sun or rising sign in Capricorn, Taurus, or Virgo. This energy encourages you to recognize and enjoy the abundance already present in your life.

Ace of Cups

Universal love

ACE OF CUPS

Ace (new beginnings) + Cups (water and emotions) = overflowing love

The Ace of Cups says that your cup runneth over! The Universe is pouring out love to you. Feel it and let it wash over you. Trust this flow of energy. As the saying goes, you can't really love another until you love yourself, so this is a good time to love and appreciate your being and let the energy of unconditional love cleanse you.

Two of Cups

Partnership

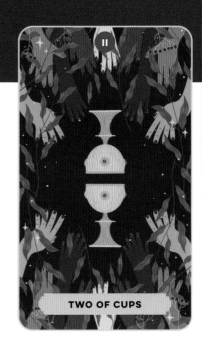

TWO OF CUPS

Two (balance) + Cups (water and emotions) = relationship

The Two of Cups is the relationship card. It indicates harmonious partnership. While The Lovers represents the overarching theme of romantic relationships, this card's energy signifies any long-term relationship. It carries the energy of really being in sync with another. You have the opportunity to share love and happiness with someone who is already in your life or entering it soon.

Three of Cups

THREE OF CUPS

Three (harmonics) + Cups (water and emotions) = sharing the love

The Three of Cups is a wonderful signifier of the celebration of love. It can point to a wedding or a gathering of friends and family that brings everyone closer together. There is an uncommon intimacy present. The depth of sharing and caring makes you feel good, and you want to express that joy to others.

Four of Cups

FOUR OF CUPS

Emotional equilibrium

Four (stability) + Cups (water and emotions) = equipoise

The Four of Cups carries an energy of detachment, but not in a negative sense. This card calls you to feel what you feel with less concern. You have an opportunity to be more meditative and simply witness your feelings. This is a good thing. You're developing equipoise—a state of equilibrium—and not getting lost in any one particular feeling.

Five of Cups

Disappointment

FIVE OF CUPS

Five (changeability) + Cups (water and emotions) = feeling pessimistic

The Five of Cups can signify disappointment. You're focused on what isn't working in your life instead of what is working. This card often has imagery of three empty cups and two full cups, with a figure focused on the empty ones. It indicates that your past disappointments are coloring your view of the present darkly. Shift your focus to the good.

Six of Cups

Nostalgia

SIX OF CUPS

Six (personal responsibility) + Cups (water and emotions) = childhood dreams

There is a quality of nostalgia to the Six of Cups—of looking back at how things were when times were good. This card carries the energy of fairy tales and fantasies about love and relationships. While generally harmless, nostalgia and wishful thinking can keep you from tapping into your own emotional reservoir right now.

Seven of Cups

SEVEN OF CUPS

Uncertainty

Seven (introspection) + Cups (water and emotions) = confusion

The Seven of Cups signifies confusing thoughts and feelings. You're a bit lost in the rain clouds. The message here is to come back to your center. Stop looking to the feelings and perspectives of others to guide your own. The tendency to reach outside of yourself for clarity just leads to more uncertainty and fear because, by doing that, you can never truly know how you feel. Bring your focus back to your own heart and feelings, and you'll see clearly.

Eight of Cups

EIGHT OF CUPS

Release

Eight (power) + Cups (water and emotions) = letting go

The Eight of Cups signifies needing to let go. We dislike releasing what has been because we fear feeling empty. Sometimes we even hold on to negative things because they feel familiar. But Cups is the suit of water and emotions. Not releasing what doesn't serve you will result in blocked emotions and stagnation. When you let your emotions keep flowing, without damming them up, they move to their ultimate destination: the sea of fulfillment.

Nine of Cups

Wishes granted

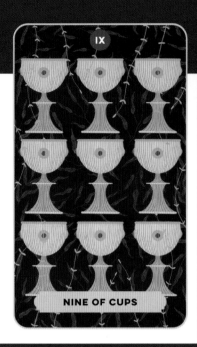

NINE OF CUPS

Nine (culmination) + Cups (water and emotions) = fulfilled desire

The Nine of Cups is the classic wish card. It indicates a time of emotional riches, when you can enjoy the satisfaction of the culmination of your desires. You will get your wish. Allow the experience of happiness, joy, and blessings to permeate your being. There's more to come, but, for now, you can bask in the feeling of fullness in your emotional life.

Ten of Cups

Abundant positivity

TEN OF CUPS

Ten (endings and new beginnings) + Cups (water and emotions) = complete harmony

The Ten of Cups heralds a time of great emotional well-being—so much so that there's plenty of good feelings to go around and share with your friends, family, and coworkers. Your heart is full and overflowing. You contain so much kindness and generosity within you that it naturally radiates out to those around you, allowing everyone to enjoy harmony. Smile and pass on the goodness!

Page of Cups

The Page of Cups is the childlike quality of the emotional self. It carries an energy of authenticity and trust in your feelings as well as the lightness of being present without self-consciousness. You know how you feel, and you are at peace with yourself. You have a sense of spaciousness as you simply follow what feels right and don't question yourself. Lean into those feelings.

PAGE OF CUPS

Page of Cups as a Person

This card signifies the experience of sweet youthful emotions. Maybe there's a child in your life who is so cute and lovable that they make everyone around them feel lighter. They carry the energy of Cancer (nurturing love), Scorpio (intense love), or Pisces (unconditional love). This water sign is just splashing around and feeling their feelings. Depending on the surrounding cards, the Page of Cups could also indicate a time of innocence and ease for yourself.

Knight of Cups

KNIGHT OF CUPS

The movement of the knight combines with deep feelings in the Knight of Cups. Desire, wishes, and longing are the hallmarks of this card. Your sexual energy is looking for expression, allowing you to make a bold move and tell someone how you feel about them. If you've ever wanted to write a love letter, now is the time.

Knight of Cups as a Person

This card can also represent a dynamic young adult with their sun or rising sign in Cancer, Scorpio, or Pisces. This person is filled with the desire to follow their heart and act on feelings of love. Depending on the placement of the card, they could be carrying a romantic torch for you or someone else. This adolescent emotional energy may also be present in yourself, no matter your age. Your emotions are stirring, and you feel frisky and adventurous. Enjoy this time of passion by feeling it in yourself or witnessing it in another.

Queen of Cups

The Queen of Cups is the feminine aspect of water—vulnerable, open, and receptive. There is great power in the feminine aspect of water because it takes a strong person to be vulnerable. This card signifies a time of emotional integrity. The queen is not being demanding or looking for reciprocity. She is simply sharing her love, compassion, and kindness. And that makes her quite beautiful to be around. This card indicates living from the heart, not the head.

Queen of Cups as a Person

This card can also indicate that a loving and nurturing woman is present or coming into your life. This could be a friend you can really trust, or maybe your mom. It could even be you. Maybe you've become more comfortable sharing your feelings. However the Queen of Cups presents herself, she carries the energy of the water signs—Cancer, Scorpio, and Pisces. This card calls you to be more open and loving with yourself.

QUEEN OF CUPS

King of Cups

KING OF CUPS

The King of Cups heralds a time of healing and emotional balance. His energy is that of a trustworthy confidant or a therapist. He has done his own work and can really understand your feelings. As the masculine aspect of the water element, this king has depth. His feelings are thoughtful, and he can share and express them in a balanced way, without fear. The King of Cups indicates that you're in a place of emotional maturity, or that it's a good time for any healing modality that will bring you to this place of inner well-being.

King of Cups as a Person

This card can also represent an adult in your life, which is good news. You can connect with this person—usually a man whose sun or rising sign may be in Cancer, Scorpio, or Pisces—on a deep level. Whether they appear in a personal relationship or in another area of your life, this is someone you can trust and open up to because they get you. They can meet you where you are emotionally. And don't we all want that kind of connection?

Ace of Swords

Inspiration

Ace (new beginnings) + Swords (air and thought) = new idea

The Ace of Swords heralds a breakthrough in thought. It's one of the few cards in this suit that's considered positive. Here, you have a lightbulb moment. A divinely inspired idea has pierced the veil of your mind. Trust it, hold on to it, and write it down so you can remember it in times of confusion.

Two of Swords

Indecision

TWO OF SWORDS

Two (balance) + Swords (air and thought) = binary thinking

The Two of Swords indicates that you're going back and forth in your mind between two ways of looking at a situation. The mind is like a computer and vacillates between zero and one—all or nothing, black or white. This limited process may have you feeling stuck. The Two of Swords calls you to tap into your feelings and intuition to get unstuck.

Three of Swords

Painful thinking

Three (harmonics) + Swords (air and thought) = negation

A classic interpretation of the Three of Swords is a kind of thinking that hurts your heart. Because thought is only logical and data driven, the realm of thinking doesn't always agree with the emotions of the heart. This card tells you that your intellect is trying to cancel out your intuition. Take this seriously because your mind, in striving for answers, thinks it's best to jettison how you feel.

THREE OF SWORDS

Four of Swords

Time out

Four (stability) + Swords (air and thought) = postponement

The Four of Swords signifies a kind of mental truce—putting a situation on pause or letting go of emotions temporarily to give yourself time to recharge and reassess. This isn't a permanent state of affairs; it's more like a coach calling for a time out to halt the action on the field and adjust the game plan. This card tells you that you may need to do this, especially if your analytical mind is running amok. Letting it rest will bring you clarity.

FOUR OF SWORDS

Five of Swords

Defeatism

Five (changeability) + Swords (air and thought) = negative comparisons

The Five of Swords carries an energy of instability, and people tend to perceive instability from a place of worry or fear. You may be looking around at others and thinking they have their act together, and you don't. Stop comparing yourself to others or to how you think you should be, and just be.

Six of Swords

Others' beliefs

Six (personal responsibility) + Swords (air and thought) = the "shoulds"

When the Six of Swords comes up in a reading, it indicates that you are carrying the thoughts and beliefs of others about how you should be feeling or living your life. These "shoulds" could be from social conditioning, your family's expectations, or even a friend's well-intentioned advice. But they are not yours. Return to your center. What do you think is right for you? What are your beliefs? This card calls for introspection.

Seven of Swords

Being true to yourself

SEVEN OF SWORDS

Seven (introspection) + Swords (air and thought) = truth

The Seven of Swords is a tricky card. It indicates that you know your truth but fear that others won't like it. You're facing a dilemma: you want it to seem like you share the same beliefs as someone else, but you don't. So, do you pretend? Or do you stand in your integrity and face the consequences? The presence of this card means it's time to do the latter.

Eight of Swords

Stubbornness

EIGHT OF SWORDS

Eight (power) + Swords (air and thought) = guilty conscience

The Eight of Swords indicates that you're in a tough place. Holding too tightly to your own attitudes without being willing to compromise has created an issue. It's possible that your need to be right took precedence over a win-win solution. Guilt is often a by-product of this energy, which can lead to further problems as it causes your mind to default to self-condemnation. Take a breath—nobody's perfect! Once you clear the air, you can move forward.

Nine of Swords

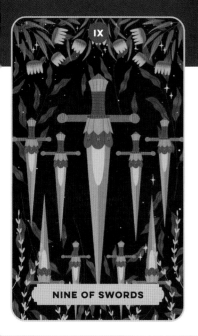

NINE OF SWORDS

Nine (culmination) + Swords (air and thought) = confronting fears

The Nine of Swords points you to your worst fears and core negative beliefs about yourself. Your mind is caught in a nightmare, and the boogeyman (your fear) is chasing you. This card tells you that, instead of running from it, it's time to turn around and face your fear. Look this scary monster in the eye and ask it what it wants. You'll find out what you need to do to release it, and it won't need to chase you anymore.

Ten of Swords

TEN OF SWORDS

Turning point

Ten (endings and new beginnings) + Swords (air and thought) = death of old beliefs

If the Ten of Swords shows up in a reading, there is an intense process at work. This card represents death and rebirth. You've hit rock bottom and can no longer sustain negativity. You're sick and tired of being sick and tired. It's become too much to manage, so you're ready to let that negativity go. Once you do, your mind can open to possibility.

Page of Swords

PAGE OF SWORDS

The Page of Swords is about playing with thought. It represents the childlike quality of letting your mind go wherever it will. There is an unbridled energy to this card. The mind just wants to flit here and there; it doesn't want to focus. So let it run around like a hyperactive kid until it wears itself out! Avoid fixating on any of your thoughts right now, and you'll find yourself settling down into a place of clarity.

Page of Swords as a Person

This card is either an aspect of yourself that you are experiencing or another person around you who just needs to vent. That might be a child or young person with their sun sign or rising sign in Gemini, Libra, or Aquarius. Their mind is curious and open. This person is interested in learning, asking questions, and processing information, but their head is all over the place. Simply allow yourself or this person to release this chaotic thinking. In other words, detach.

Knight of Swords

The knight's need to move, combined with the velocity of the mental realm, usually produces combativeness in the Knight of Swords. There's a tendency to come out of the gate fighting for your ideas or beliefs, even when you aren't really attached to them. Chances are, something has triggered a defensive posture in you. The ghosts of past battles have reared their heads, and you think you have to fight old fights all over again. Don't believe everything you think right now.

KNIGHT OF SWORDS

Knight of Swords as a Person

When the Knight of Swords shows up, someone is being a hothead—check and see if it's you! If so, go out for a run or get in the car and hit the freeway so you can move something besides your mind. This card can also represent a young person in your life whose sun or rising sign is in Gemini, Libra, or Aquarius. This person has that twenty-something vigor and believes in their cause and their own perspective too strongly. Their mind is set on something, and they will keep investigating until they have their answers. They need to convince you of their opinion. If you disagree, just nod and let them advocate for their ideas until the energy dissipates.

Queen of Swords

QUEEN OF SWORDS

The Queen of Swords is the feminine aspect of air. She has certain ideas about how things should be and feels the need to help others by telling them what she thinks they should do. Advice and counsel are the hallmarks of this this card. The Queen means well, but check in with yourself and see whether her beliefs hold true for you.

Queen of Swords as a Person

This card can also represent someone in your life (usually a woman) whose sun or rising sign is in Gemini, Libra, or Aquarius. This person prizes intellectual prowess above all else. They're convinced that they have the right perspective—and they may! The Queen of Swords can also signify your mother or the belief system that comes down through the maternal line. If this applies to you, it might be a good time for a reality check on your own belief systems.

King of Swords

The King of Swords is the masculine aspect of the element of air. He represents logic and disciplined thinking. This card's energy is good for getting organized and setting a schedule. But be warned: the authoritative quality present here can easily turn into authoritarianism. This card represents the mastery of thought—you might think you know and can control everything. Are you *too* disciplined? Are you shutting out other aspects of yourself in the name of logic (i.e., your intuition)? This card reminds you that the analytical mind is just one aspect of consciousness.

KING OF SWORDS

King of Swords as a Person

This is a highly patriarchal card. It can represent a man in your life who is either your father or is acting like it. He carries the energy of Gemini, Libra, or Aquarius. The King of Swords wears the pants in the family. He's used to being listened to. He can be right, but he is also controlling, and that's something to watch out for. If this is someone in your life, "you're not the boss of me" would be a good mantra to adopt now. But also be mindful of this controlling aspect in yourself: the inner critic.

PART 3

PUTTING THINGS *into* PERSPECTIVE

The Importance of Synthesis

Before we look at the various spreads, let's focus on synthesis—aka reading the cards in relation to each other. One of the most challenging aspects of doing a Tarot reading is bringing the messages of each card together with its placement in a spread. Starting with a basic understanding of the placements will help.

Within each spread, the center card will always represent the core message. It gives you insight into where you are now. A one-card reading is just about this core message; in multiple-card spreads, the other cards add to the core message. This is why understanding the positioning of the cards is so vital—it makes a huge difference whether the other cards are in the past or future position.

The past is always to the left of the center card and the future is always to the right in any spread with more than one card. As you might guess, the past position indicates where you've been. Whichever card comes up in that placement gives you information about how your past experience affects the central message. Depending on the suit, this could refer to a specific event, or it could have more to do with emotional or psychological awareness. And a major arcana card in this position indicates an overarching theme that you've been working with for some time.

A card in the future position indicates where you're headed. It shows your trajectory based on the central message. Always interpret the future card with the past card in mind, because where you're coming from colors how you see the future. Depending on the suit, a minor card appearing in this position could indicate an emotional bias (Cups) or psychological perspective (Swords), actions you've taken in the past (Wands), or some material situation (Pentacles). A major arcana card in the future position tells you that you're entering a situation that has more long-lasting ramifications.

Keep Some Perspective

Because most people come to Tarot looking for guidance about the future, any card in the future position can feel daunting. But it's important to see its message as part of a continuum. Nothing is set in stone. Even if the card in this position is negative, it's just giving you information. We can never know exactly how these energies will manifest, so approaching a reading with detachment and objectivity is key.

Once you understand the placements themselves, you need to understand the relationship between them. In a three-card spread, for example, you would ask yourself how the card in the past position brings you to the central theme occurring now. Then you would think about how that relationship affects the future card. When you bring more than one card into a reading, a kind of alchemy occurs between the cards—the whole is worth more than the sum of its parts.

As you get into spreads involving more cards and thus more placements, the information you get becomes more detailed. Take the time to study the placements of each spread (explained in the following sections) before looking at the cards. This will go a long way toward keeping your readings accurate.

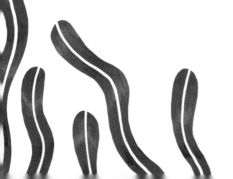

Understanding the Layouts

From the simple one-card reading to the classic Celtic Cross spread, you'll find a variety of layouts to help you get the information you need. And, over time, you'll master them all. You'll understand just which one to use in a reading, know the placements by heart, and easily interpret the cards in relation to one another. But you need to take things one step at a time as you're learning.

Start by getting familiar with the layouts themselves. Interpreting the cards gets easier when you understand a spread's placements—it helps you avoid confusion and information overload during an actual reading. In the following pages, you'll find diagrams of each of the spreads. Before you try doing a reading, look at the layout of the spread you'll be working with. This is the framework for your reading. Study it. Notice how the cards are placed and what meaning each position holds. You only need to remember a keyword or two for each placement. With this knowledge under your belt, you'll see the pattern inherent in each layout. Then you can synthesize the relationships between the card placements. And within that context, the individual cards in a reading begin to tell a story.

Think about building a house. You pour the foundation first, then the framing goes up. Only after that can you install the plumbing and electrical systems. Next comes the drywall, which completes the walls and ceiling. Then you can begin to see the house for what it really is. In Tarot, you create your foundation by first understanding the significance of each card's placement in a layout. You then frame your reading by laying out the cards. Next, you begin to make connections between them (the

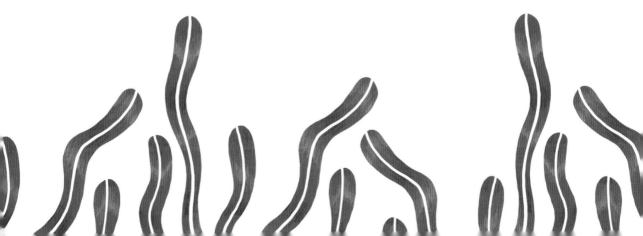

plumbing and electrical). Finally, you interpret the cards, filling in the structure with details to create a fuller picture.

Remember that having a foundational understanding of each layout is the basis for accurate interpretation. One of the biggest mistakes a Tarot reader can make is misunderstanding the placement of a card, but you can easily avoid that. Just take your time and study the outlines of the spreads before you use them. Once you've learned the basic meanings of each card in a spread, you can try your hand at a reading.

Start by practicing only one-card readings for a while. Then, as you become more proficient, practice three-card spreads. When you feel comfortable interpreting the relationships between the cards, you can move on to more complex layouts. By the time you get to the Celtic Cross—the most comprehensive layout we'll cover—you'll be a virtual master at pattern recognition.

With that in mind, we'll begin with the simplest layout and work up to the most comprehensive one. Not only will you learn about the placements within the layouts, you'll also get a feeling for the ritual of Tarot reading. Once we cement that foundation, we'll work on using everything you've learned about the cards, layouts, and your own intuition to connect the dots and fill in the details.

Less Is More

The general rule here is *less is more*. There is a tendency to think that pulling more cards in a reading will give you more information. While that's true in a certain context (pulling a clarifying card in the Celtic Cross spread, for example), it usually has a watering-down effect on the cards' guidance. It's better to go deeper into each card's meaning within a layout— this is what will reveal more information. Pulling cards unnecessarily creates more confusion, causing you to lose that depth of insight.

✳ THE ONE-CARD READING ✳

The one-card reading is very useful for when you have a specific question and want answers about one thing. It's also helpful for learning the cards in their context. A good practice when you're starting out is to pull one card every day. Think of this as your morning meditation—a time for tuning into your intuition.

    This one card carries a lot of information, both symbolic and energetic. By using this practice every day, you'll strengthen not only your own internal guidance system but also your understanding of the cards, which will help you quickly become adept at reading Tarot. Treat it like any other, more complex spread by exploring every detail of the card as having the potential to add to its interpretation.

✳ THE THREE-CARD SPREAD ✳

The three-card spread offers a bit more context than the one-card spread. In this layout, the first card—appropriately placed in the center—identifies the central message. Give this card precedence in your reading. The second card, which you place to the left of the first, indicates where you're coming from and what you've already experienced that has led you to the central card. And the third card, which you place to the right of the first, is where you're headed.

This spread allows you to see the bigger picture of what's going on with you or someone you're reading for. It's simple but powerful because it gives the reading more scope and shows you a trajectory. Use it to see how your past has affected your current life situation and how these messages are pointing you toward the meaning of the future card.

2 PAST

1 CORE MESSAGE

3 FUTURE

✳ THE V SPREAD ✳

The V Spread is best for when you have a specific question or issue and need more comprehensive guidance than the three-card spread provides. It breaks information into bite-size pieces, offering more nuance and greater perspective. Seeing each step along the way to your outcome gives you the information you need to decide whether you're on the right track or need to make a change.

This layout involves seven cards focused on a central theme, which is represented by the card at the point of the V (card number 4). The left arm of the V reflects where you're coming from up to where you are now. The right arm of the V gives you information about your future trajectory and the influences around you.

To lay out the cards, place the first card faceup at the top left point of the V. Lay the second card at an angle beneath the first card. Repeat this with the third card, continuing to angle the cards down toward the point of the V. Place the fourth card at that point. The fifth card goes to the right at an upward angle. Repeat with the sixth and seventh cards to complete the V.

In a reading, begin with the cards on the left. The top left card (card number 1) represents the past, the middle left (card number 2) represents the recent past, and the bottom left (card number 3) represents where you are now. Think of them as three steps that have led you to the central card and its message. You'll want to see how the three steps of the left hand cards are related to the guidance of that central card.

Once you feel clear about the overall messages so far, move on to the three cards on the right arm of the V. The card just to the right of the central card (card number 5) reflects your environment in the near future (you may even sense its energy in the present). This placement gives you information about your surroundings and how they will affect you.

The next card (card number 6) reflects your hopes and fears regarding your question. The card in this placement indicates what you expect in the situation you're inquiring about. This is important, because we tend to get what we expect. So if this card reflects something that you don't want, you know what to change about your expectations. If the card carries positive energy, it's affirming that you're on the right path.

The card at the top of the right arm of the V (card number 7) represents the general outcome of the situation. (Remember, this isn't set in stone.) In a reading, notice the relationship between the theme of the central card and the outcome. Then look back on the cards representing your environment and your expectations. Those two cards are literally pointing to the outcome, showing you how your environment and your underlying expectations may be influencing the results.

By using the placements to understand how you got here and where you're going, you can take control of the situation. That's what makes layouts like the V spread so helpful—they offer greater depth and breadth of information for tackling more complex questions.

1 PAST INFLUENCES

2 RECENT PAST

3 PRESENT

4 CORE MESSAGE

5 SURROUNDING INFLUENCES

6 HOPES AND FEARS

7 OUTCOME

It's critical to remember that Tarot, with its powerful symbolism, is a tool for guidance and self-reflection. The messages in the cards are not set in stone. They are simply mirroring a process going on within you. Each reading is a manifestation of your intuition speaking to you about where you are, based on the past, and how you are poised toward the future. And knowledge is power. Eighty percent of the work you do to create change is understanding and gaining awareness of the situation. The rest is putting that awareness to good use.

✳ THE RELATIONSHIP SPREAD ✳

Humans are relational beings, which means our relationships are vital to our lives and well-being. So a spread that helps you gain insight into and awareness about your relationships is essential. The Relationship Spread does just that. With four cards, this layout shows you where you're coming from, what's going on with the other person, the energy between the two of you, and general guidance for your relationship. Use it to help you understand the dynamics present in any relationship.

In a reading, you'll visualize the person you want guidance about (or have your subject do the same) before you shuffle the deck. Once they're clear in your mind's eye, see them connected, grounded, and protected in a column of white light. As you shuffle the cards, ask your question or ask that the highest guidance come through about this relationship.

Create a square layout with four cards, faceup, as follows: Pull the top card from the deck and place it in front of you. Lay the second card to the right of the first card.

Pull the third card from the deck and place it below the first card. Place the fourth card to the right of the third card (below the second).

The top left placement (card number 1) represents you. The card to the right of it (card number 2) represents the other person. This guidance tells you about what's going on for them regarding the interaction between you two. The card at the bottom left (card number 3) represents the energy present between you and this person. And the card to the bottom right (card number 4) represents the guidance for you about this relationship. In this layout, the fourth card offers the core message for the reading.

It may feel strange to work with the card placement that signifies the other person—as if you're a peeping Tom, secretly observing them. If you come to this process with the intention of true understanding and awareness, you have nothing to worry about. But if you come at this like a chess game, trying to find a strategy to manipulate the other person, you won't get far. The spread's guidance will fall by the wayside, and you'll end up more confused than when you started. Intention is key. If your intention is always seeking insight for the highest good, that's what you'll get. And the clarity, peace, and awareness you'll get with that intention will benefit not only you but the other person as well.

The first two cards show you the energy that you and the other person are bringing to the relationship at this time, while the third card represents the energy around the two of you together. These placements give you a greater understanding of the fourth card's guidance, allowing you to put things into perspective. This can show you what's working or where you need to make a change.

In a reading, consider the energy you're bringing to the situation (card number 1). Does it enhance your awareness of your position? When you look at the card representing the other person, can you understand them a little better? Can you appreciate where they are, energetically, and what they may be experiencing?

Bring these questions to the third card, which represents the alchemy between you and the other person. What is the energy between you? If it's negative, go deeper. How can this awareness help you shift your perspective so you can effect positive change in your life? The fourth card holds the key. It's telling you what *you* can do. We can't change other people (although many try!). We only have control over ourselves and our own reactions. But we can grow in our own awareness and apply that clarity to our relationships, often helping to change their dynamic for the better.

The relationship spread tends to elicit strong emotional responses. Feel your way through this process, keeping your analytical mind at bay. Remember that you're simply seeking awareness and understanding, so try to stay as neutral as possible. You may find yourself disagreeing with the card that represents you. But you came to Tarot, and to this particular spread, looking for insight. Maybe it will confirm what you already feel, and maybe it won't. Stay open! Bring a beginner's mind to this reading and try to be as objective as possible. It's all just energy. Try not to think of it as "right or wrong" or "good or bad." There are always helpful lessons to be found if you're open to finding them.

Keep an Open Mind

It's vitally important to keep an open mind when using the relationship spread. It carries the potential to change how you feel about your relationships. It might even help you realize when yours has passed its expiration date. If that's the case, this spread can then help you understand why you came together and the lessons the other person brought into your life.

✳ THE CELTIC CROSS ✳

The Celtic Cross is the classic Tarot spread. It's one that most professional Tarot readers use because it offers a wide-angle view of a person's life at the present time rather than the telephoto focus of smaller spreads centered on a specific question. They can see the big picture around a person and offer more guidance.

This basic formation of ten cards gives you a comprehensive look at where you are now, what you've recently come from, and how the future is stacking up. You'll see that if you (or the person you're reading for) need more information later, you can add cards to the spread. But it's best to lay out the ten placements and work with those first. There's a lot of information to be had in this spread, and it takes time to process it all.

Because this is a large layout, you'll need plenty of space to do this spread. Although it's a good idea to get a general impression of the whole layout, working one section at a time will help you avoid overwhelm. So let's start with the cross pattern (the first six cards).

Card number 1, the center card, gives you guidance about yourself and/or the situation you're in. Card number 2 represents what's either aiding you or inhibiting you, depending on the card. If it's positive, then you're being supported by this energy. If it's negative, this indicates an obstacle or something to work on. Either way, the card in this placement shows you what you can shift right now.

Card number 3 represents your conscious perspective at this time, giving you information about where your head is. Card number 4 gives you insight into your subconscious thoughts, which can be very helpful, as we so often operate from our subconscious motivations without knowing it. This placement indicates your underlying perspective. In a reading, notice whether it's very different from the card in the conscious position. These first four cards give you a lot of information about what your situation is presently.

Next, zoom out and look at linear time. The card on the left (card number 5) indicates the recent past, giving you insight into how your past is influencing your present situation. Think about how this card corresponds with the first four cards. Card number 6, sitting to the right of the central column, shows how you're poised to move forward in the near future.

10

OUTCOME
(CORE
MESSAGE)

3

CONSCIOUS
THOUGHTS

9

HOPES AND
FEARS

5

RECENT PAST

2

OBSTACLE OR
OPPORTUNITY

6

NEAR
FUTURE

8

OUTER
INFLUENCES

1: THE SITUATION

4

UNCONSCIOUS
THOUGHTS

7

FUTURE

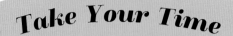

Take Your Time

The Celtic Cross spread is one of the most well-known and widely used spreads in Tarot. But it can also one of the most difficult to learn, with ten or more cards per reading. This is a lot of data to process. You could stare at this spread for a few hours and still come up with new insights. So take it easy. If you feel frustrated or confused, slow down. If you're unclear about the answers, sit with the questions a little longer. You may even want to take a picture of the whole spread and refer back to it after a few days with fresh eyes. Often, taking space is the best thing you can do.

Once you've thoroughly examined the six cards of the cross pattern, it's time to move forward. Card number 6 acts as a bridge between all the energy and influences present and how they'll position you for the future. The vertical line made up of the last four cards represents what's to come.

Card number 7, which represents the future, is essentially the stance you'll take based on where you are now. As you move up the line to the card number 8, you'll learn about outer influences. Whether it speaks to the personal or professional sphere, this position indicates your future surroundings and how they may impact you. A card that indicates supportive influences is great. But a card that indicates negative influences can act as a helpful heads-up. The future will be what you make it.

The next card up the ladder, card number 9, represents your hopes and fears for the future—in other words, your expectations. Remember, we tend to get what we expect. So if this card reflects something that you don't want, it could indicate that you need a change.

Finally, the top card in the line (card number 10) offers the key guidance about the outcome of your situation. It shows you the results produced by the combination of where you are now, your future trajectory, and your influences and expectations. As you look over the vertical column of four cards, can you see a pattern? What story are these cards and their positions telling you?

Although the outcome position represents the key guidance in this spread, it's still only one of ten cards. So resist the urge to put too much weight on it in a reading. Your readings will be more accurate and helpful when you remember to always consider context. With that in mind, finish your reading with a complete recapitulation of the entire Celtic Cross spread. Scan each card in order from the first to the tenth to see if any more impressions arise. Reread the entire trajectory from start to finish and notice if there are any gaps in the continuity of the story. If there are, spend more time with the surrounding cards. Allow your intuition to show you any pieces that you may have overlooked. This is like following a trail of breadcrumbs; if you skip one, you will go astray. And each of those breadcrumbs gives you valuable information about your situation and insight you can act on.

Clarifying Cards

If the final card in a Celtic Cross reading concerns you, confuses you, or seems anticlimactic, then this is the time to pull another card from the top of the deck. Place it faceup to the left of card number 10. This card can clarify card number 10's guidance about your outcome by showing you what's possible. Now pull another card and place it faceup to the right of card number 10. This indicates another possibility. Adding these cards can show you a fork in the road, requiring a choice, or can enhance the initial card's message. They don't supersede card number 10; they're simply an addendum.

Pulling It All Together

We've covered the card meanings and learned about the various layouts and definitions of each placement. So now we get to the fun part—putting it all together! With a basic understanding of how the pieces come together, you can start doing readings for yourself and others. After all, the only way to get good at doing something is to start doing it. This may feel a bit daunting, but you'll see that all the different aspects of reading Tarot coalesce with study and practice.

In any reading, your intention is key. Because Tarot was historically used as a divination tool, many people come to readings looking to predict the future. This is a precarious way to approach a reading. First, remember that Tarot is essentially a book of symbolism. The cards don't have any magical power; they're a tool we use to expand our own awareness. Second, we can only draw meaning from the cards using what we know, which is based on our own experiences and how we've interpreted them. In readings and in life, we extrapolate ahead based on where we are and where we've been. That means we see the future from our own limited perspective. But we can do better than predict the future. By keeping an open and curious mind, we can tap into our intuition and use the cards' symbolic guidance to *create* our future.

✳ ESTABLISHING A RITUAL ✳

Before you begin working with the cards, establish a ritual for your practice. You'll use this ritual to begin each reading, as well as while you're learning the layouts. It should include creating a sacred space for your reading, connecting to a higher power, breathing deeply, setting an intention, and holding your intention while you shuffle the cards.

Create a sacred space. Pick a place where you can sit quietly. You may want to start each reading by lighting a candle, which invites the light into your reading. It's also a good idea to clear the energy in your space, which you can do by burning cleansing herbs or incense, or by visualizing the space bathed in white light.

Connect to higher guidance. Once you've established the setting, you need to connect to higher guidance. This part of the ritual can vary from person to person, depending on their spiritual beliefs. If you want to keep it simple, use the "connect, ground, protect" exercise on page 33 to connect to Source energy. Sit up straight, with your feet on the floor and legs uncrossed. See the column of white light coming down from above, encapsulating you and then going deep into the earth.

Breathe deeply. When you feel connected, take three deep breaths. Inhaling through the nose and exhaling through the mouth signals the brain to go into relaxation mode, helping to release tension and calm the nervous system (a good practice to use anytime!). By connecting to Source and relaxing, you're shifting your energy out of "normal mode." This process acts as a mini meditation to create a feeling of spaciousness, prepare you to receive intuitive guidance, and activate the subtle senses.

Set your intention. The next step is very important: set the intention for the reading. An intention is a clear objective. The basic intention of any Tarot reading is to receive guidance, accessing perspective and insight beyond your normal consciousness. You can't go wrong by simply asking for the highest guidance to come through. But you may also have a specific situation in mind. In that case, your intention might take the form of a question or a request for guidance about that particular situation (e.g., clarity about a relationship). If you believe in angels, or spiritual helpers and guides, this is a good time to ask that they come forth to assist with the reading.

Shuffle the cards. Try not to overthink your shuffle. Simply hold your intention in your mind, shuffle until you feel finished, and then use your left hand to cut the deck into three piles. Again using your left hand, put the cards back into one pile, facedown, in any order. Always keep the cards facedown while shuffling. When you read for someone else, you'll have them shuffle the deck. But we'll cover reading for other people a little later, on page 145.

Storing Your Cards

Some people like to keep their Tarot cards in a silk scarf or a special pouch. Keeping the cards in something other than the box they came in makes your relationship with your cards more personal. It also helps to create some distance between you and the author of the deck. Of course, there's nothing wrong with the author and their interpretations (which you'll usually find in a small leaflet bundled with your cards). But there will come a point when your intuition will combine with those interpretations to create something new. You may find that the guidance you receive about a particular card differs from the author's. Trust yourself and the guidance you receive.

✳ INTERPRETING A LAYOUT ✳

Start with your ritual, settling into your space and setting your intention. You should also have a journal or notebook and pen handy to write down your impressions as they come to you. This is a habit that will help you as you learn how to interpret the cards as well as when you're doing readings. You'll be asking yourself a lot of questions and covering a lot of information, and your thoughts will come quickly. Keeping a notebook helps you capture them all.

When you're ready, begin to lay out the cards. Slowly and methodically pull the first card off the top of the pile and place it faceup in the first position indicated by your chosen spread. Repeat this for each card and placement until you've laid out the entire spread.

To interpret the cards, you'll begin by softening your gaze and allowing your intuition to take the lead. Once you've finished noting all of your initial impressions, you'll move on to studying the cards. Remember, you're not only reading each card, you're also analyzing their placements and their relationships to each other.

Take It All In

Once you have all your cards laid out, soften your gaze (rest your eyes at a downward angle and let them remain unfocused) and look over the spread. Write down your initial impressions. Which cards jump out at you? There are always certain cards in a layout that will grab your attention. Write down anything that comes to you about them. Then begin to ask yourself questions: What is the central theme of the reading? Are there major arcana cards? What are they and where are they located in the layout? Are there a lot of minor arcana cards in one suit? If so, that element is giving you a message about the area of life you are focused on (or need to focus on). Let the cards speak to you. And do *not* overthink it.

Reversed Cards

If a card comes up in the reversed position, meaning that the image is upside-down, turn it right-side up before setting it down. There's no need to attribute a different meaning to reversed Tarot cards; the symbolism inherent in each card is enough. The messages in every card are there to support you. Guidebooks with the classical decks do give reversed meanings, but these complicate the definitions of each card unnecessarily and usually present a negative interpretation of the card. Would you hang a painting on the wall upside down? Probably not. That would distort the artist's intention. The same goes with Tarot cards. Maintain the integrity of the images on each card by placing it right-side up.

Focus on Each Card

Next, focus on each card individually, noting your impressions as you do. Begin with the first card you placed in the layout and work your way through the rest in numerical order. But always keep in mind the central card in a spread—the one that holds the core message.

As you look at a card, what is your first reaction? Do you feel fear? Happiness? Excitement? Confusion? Note any emotions that come up. Then sit back and soften your gaze again. This both quiets the mind and allows the energy of the images to come through. What's the first thing you notice visually about the card? Which senses does it evoke? Colors or certain parts of the imagery might jump out at you.

While still in this place of reflection, write down the card's name and your initial impressions in your Tarot journal. Then begin to dig deeper. What do you feel? Write down at least five descriptive words. What do you hear? Write down at least five sounds that come to you. What do you see? Write down at least five impressions. Do any words spring to mind? Do certain emotions arise? Just let the information flow.

Study the Many Facets

Next, pick up each card and study it. You want to take the card's meaning into consideration, of course, but you should never stop there. Explore all the aspects of the card that could add to its interpretation, beginning with its placement. Context is extremely important when interpreting each card. Keep that in mind as you note your impressions.

A major arcana card indicates a powerful theme in your life right now or an energy that will be with you for some time. This energy is part of the collective unconscious, not just personal to you. It's a product of the information that we've picked up from our conditioning, other people, and the world around us. Consider how these outside influences have affected your situation.

If the card is a minor arcana card, make a note of its suit. This will tell you whether the main message relates to your thoughts (Swords), emotional life (Cups), actions (Wands), or material reality (Pentacles). If it's a numbered card, consider the meaning of that number. And if it's a court card, note the characteristics of the person it represents. Can you identify it as a characteristic in yourself at this time? Do you get a sense that it represents another person in your life? Can you think of someone who embodies the characteristics of this card?

Consider the imagery of the card and its symbolism as well. Does the card feel positive or negative? Remember, all information is valuable. Whether a card is positive or negative, it gives you insight you can use. If the card is negative, you can always adjust your perspective and shift your expectations to the positive. (You'll learn more about the value of negative cards starting on page 136.) When you're finished, set the card back down and write down any other impressions you have about its energy, including any patterns you notice.

Practice Makes Proficient

Reading Tarot is like anything else—practice builds proficiency. You're strengthening the intuition muscle. The conscious practice of stepping back from your analytical mind to allow your inner guidance to come through will become easier. The more you practice, the more you'll find yourself achieving greater awareness of the overall patterns in your life. This is the reward, because what we see, we can change. And that builds an inner certainty that we do have power and can effect *positive* change. But it always comes from the inside out.

Understand the Alchemy

Once you've written down what initially came to you about each card, sit back and study the combination of the cards and the alchemy it creates. Think of each card in relation to the core message of the spread and the intention you set. These cards are telling a story—their combination gives you insight into a process. If the spread includes cards in past and future placements, explore how they inform and relate to each other. In larger layouts, such as the V spread, try looking at that story one chapter at a time—past, present, and future—before considering the larger tale.

Take a breath and return to your question. Look over what you've written down about the impressions that have come to you. Can you see a pattern? Are there multiple suits or just one? Is there more than one major arcana card? Allow the pieces of information to come together as you observe the overall picture. Resist the urge to make everything fit neatly into a specific narrative. Let it be more of a watercolor painting than a detailed drawing.

The Protein of the Message

If you find yourself feeling a bit lost or confused, return to the central card. As in the one-card reading, this card offers the most important guidance—the protein of your answer. Think of the other cards as the veggies, sauce, and side dishes (just to stick with the metaphor). They fill out the meal and add to your experience, but the protein is the main event.

If the central card and/or the future card in a spread are major arcana, then this is a strong message about the greater themes present in your life. It also indicates a longer process to work through. Take time to consider what these themes mean for you right now.

If your reading includes mostly minor arcana cards, then the situation you're facing is of a much more temporal nature. That doesn't mean it's not important, but the energies reflected in the reading are short-term and can be changed quickly. They could relate to a specific way of thinking (Swords), an emotional experience (Cups), a practical matter (Pentacles), or a recent action (Wands). You should also note whether the trajectory from the past to the future is positive or negative. A positive trajectory might show clarity or peace, for example. But not all trajectories are positive. If yours is negative, it also offers very useful guidance. In fact, the seemingly negative cards are often the most helpful. They give you a chance to understand the influences present in your life and adjust them. This is true for all suits, but especially for the Swords and the Cups. They mirror your thinking and feeling states, respectively, and you can shift the way you think and feel to a great degree. But you can also adjust your actions (Wands) and how you handle your material life (Pentacles) to produce a more desirable outcome. (For more information on so-called positive and negative cards, see page 136.)

If there's a preponderance of positive cards, then it's a sign that you're on a good track. The Universe may be trying to cheer you on. Take heart that there's a lot of positive energy in your life, and keep on keeping on.

An Interpretation Checklist

There are a lot of nuances in any reading, but here's a general list of things to look and feel for as you interpret the cards.

☐ First impressions
☐ Notable cards
☐ The energy of each card
☐ The energy of the cards collectively
☐ Each card's meaning
☐ Each card's placement
☐ Each card's placement relative to the other placements
☐ Major arcana vs. minor arcana
☐ Suit and its elements
☐ Numbers or court card
☐ Art and colors
☐ Symbolism
☐ Positive or negative
☐ Relationship between the cards

Performing Tarot Readings

You've learned how to tap into your intuition, how to interpret the cards, and how to put everything into context. All that's left to do is an actual reading! This section covers the specifics of doing a reading for another person and for yourself, but let's start with a few more tips for receiving the highest guidance in a reading. If you're new to the practice, these will set you up for success. If you're an experienced practitioner, then this information will just add to your process.

✳ TIPS TO GUIDE YOUR READINGS ✳

Being in the right headspace before you begin a reading makes all the difference. That's part of the reason you establish a pre-reading ritual—you need to prepare your mind to receive the highest guidance. And there are a few more things you can do to help with that. The first is to be fully present and open to receiving the guidance. That seems like a no-brainer, but it can be tricky. Second, let your intuition take the lead in a reading before turning the interpretations over to the logical brain. And learn to appreciate all of the guidance the cards offer—negative, positive, and everything in between. It all serves a purpose. Finally, understand that time is flexible. The cards and their placements in a reading offer a rough timeline, but things can always change.

Be Open to Change

If we don't change our negative thoughts and behaviors, we can't get to better results. Doing the same thing over and over and expecting a different result isn't just the definition of insanity, it's also a waste of time. If you want a different result, you have to do things differently. As long as you're open to its guidance, Tarot can help you pinpoint what needs to change and show you what's possible when you change it.

Objectivity Is Key

Your job when doing a reading is to step out of linear time and look at things as objectively as possible. Generally, this is easiest to do when reading for someone you don't know well—you won't have many preconceived notions about them and their situation. It takes more discipline to read for someone you know, and even more detachment to read for yourself. This is why learning how to quiet your logical, analytical mind is essential. It's also why we'll cover reading for others before diving into reading for yourself. But every reading benefits from the right approach.

It's essential to approach all cards in Tarot with neutrality and equanimity. The goal is to use the cards to gain awareness, objectivity, and guidance. But we're emotional, reactive beings. We carry the weight of past disappointments, survival mechanisms, and strategies that we've used to get through various circumstances. That's a lot of baggage to bring to any situation.

Imagine you're traveling overseas to begin a new chapter in your life. You're looking for more freedom, ease of movement, and a chance to express who you are in the world. You've already started the process by choosing your destination and embarking on the journey. But you arrive at the airport with six suitcases of belongings.

Not only will that amount of baggage cost you a fortune in fees, it will also weigh you down. But you worry that you might need something you can't get at your destination. So you've overpacked and are now burdened with all these things. You don't need all that stuff. Let it go and focus on enjoying the journey. You'll find that you don't need nearly as much as you thought.

This is how you want to approach a reading, whether for another person or for yourself—light on the baggage! Try to set all of your beliefs, fears, prejudices, and expectations aside and be fully present and open to the journey that each reading takes you on. You can't control the expectations and beliefs that another person brings to their reading, but you're their tour guide, not their porter. Don't pick up their baggage and lug it with you. Of course you have empathy, but it doesn't serve your querent (the person you're reading for) to comply with their agenda. Maintain your objectivity.

Go with the Flow

Seeing Cups (the suit of emotions and water) in a reading can be a good reminder to let go and lighten up. Emotions seem to have a life of their own, but they're intimately linked with our thoughts. Test this theory out: Think of a happy memory. How do you feel? Now think of a hurtful situation. How do you feel? You'll notice that your thoughts can change your emotions. And just as the water element needs to keep moving to avoid being stagnant, we need to avoid getting stuck in our feelings. "Go with the flow" isn't just a cute saying; it's imperative. If we allow our feelings to simply move through us without damming them up, we can move through life's vicissitudes with more ease and grace. And we can let go of what's no longer serving us to see life—and the cards—with fresh eyes.

From Intuition to Information

The best way to begin a reading is by accessing your intuition. Your intuition operates outside of linear space and time; it has no boundaries. So tapping into your inner guidance gives you the opportunity to receive information beyond your memories of the past and projections into the future.

Once you've engaged your intuition, just open up. If you're reading for yourself, write down your impressions. If you're reading for someone else, just start talking. Let your right brain (the creative side) take the wheel and your intuition speak through you, stream-of-consciousness style. Because you're in an altered state created by the ritual of connecting to Source, you're basically channeling. Don't worry—you're not channeling some otherworldly entity. You're simply allowing higher guidance to come through you.

After you've expressed everything about your initial intuitive perceptions, then you can let the left brain (the logical side) weigh in on the meanings of the cards. This is the time to use your understanding of the cards and the context of their positions to fill in the details and connect the dots. But resist the urge to tie up the story of the reading into a nice little bow. Keep the process open and fluid as you go, and you'll find that the advice inherent in the messages of the cards will be more accurate.

Appreciating All Guidance

We've touched on so-called positive and negative cards before, but now it's time for a deep dive into the concept. The number-one rule of thumb is that *all* cards are there to provide guidance. What we would consider the negative cards are often the most helpful because they point directly to what you can change. So are they really negative? You may want to ponder the philosophical implications of that question!

In Tibetan Buddhism, there's something known as a *wrathful deity*. It's often portrayed as an ugly monster with its tongue out and its teeth dripping blood. It's not sweet, peaceful, or benevolent looking, but it is an aspect of the Divine. That's because it's there to help. Some wrathful deities are said to protect against demons. Others are

there to protect us from ourselves and our own egos. Their modus operandi is to scare you—to eat up and spit out some part of you that's holding you back.

Think of the scary-looking major arcana cards such as Death, The Tower, and The Devil as wrathful deities. And imagine what are classically considered the negative minor arcana cards (most of the Swords, for example) as the wrathful deities' minions. They're like the Wicked Witch of the West and her creepy flying monkeys in *The Wizard of Oz*. And how does Dorothy defeat the Wicked Witch? With water—a symbol of intuition and the pure power of feeling. When you think of it that way, the witch doesn't seem all that scary.

With that in mind, we're going to use the terms "negative" and "positive" loosely as we take a closer look at the guidance the cards offer. The goal is to approach all cards and their meanings objectively, without judgment or fear. That way, you can glean the helpful message that each of these cards offers.

Every Negative Can Become a Positive

Let's say you get the Ten of Swords—a card meaning acute fear—in a reading. This card shows you that you're perceiving your reality in a deeply fearful way. Instead of letting this card add to your fear, stop and recognize what this fear is. Like the card itself, the fear is just a signal to become conscious of your thoughts so you can change them. Reprogram your thinking by replacing the fear with its opposite. Negative thoughts are not more accurate than positive ones—they are just more common!

The Negative Cards

Let's look at the negative cards first, particularly those of the minor arcana. The suit of Swords has the most negative cards, followed by the suits of Cups, Wands, and, lastly, Pentacles. As the suit that includes the most seemingly negative cards, we'll spend a little extra time on Swords.

Swords. This suit represents thinking and belief systems. If you spoke every thought that went through your mind for one hour into an audio recorder and then played the audio back for yourself, you might be shocked by the negativity. This doesn't mean you're a negative person—it just means that, as human beings, we tend to place more weight on negative thoughts (called *negativity bias*). So thoughts tinged with fear, doubt, worry, agitation, frustration, judgment, and self-condemnation tend to perpetuate.

There's also an energetic reason that these negative thoughts are so pervasive. Remember that Swords also represent the ephemeral element of air. Like radio waves, thoughts hang in the air, imperceptibly surrounding us, until they find a receiver. The atmosphere is full of them, and our minds act as the receivers for them. Although we imagine all of our thoughts to be original and self-made, many come to us from outside sources. And the beliefs we pick up in childhood (when the brain is the most sponge-like) from our families, schools, friends, and society make up so much of what we think. In other words, your mind is full of thoughts that have been around for eons. So don't take them too personally.

If Swords come up in a reading, the cards are simply saying that it's time to look at your thoughts. Then you can gain awareness and change your thinking from negative, limiting beliefs to positive, expansive beliefs. (*Whew!* That clears the air.)

Cups. The suit of Cups represents the emotional realm. It can indicate some negative feelings such as disappointment, defensiveness, and grief. Again, all the messages in Tarot are there to help. If you see Cups in a reading, the cards are simply pointing to these emotions so that you can understand and release them.

Wands. The suit of Wands represents action. It's easy to see how overexertion or a lack of focused action can be perceived as negative. Wands arise in a reading to bring our attention to these situations so we can adjust, slow down, and take care of ourselves.

Pentacles. Because the suit of Pentacles represents the earth element and material issues, its negative cards have to do with hanging on too tightly to our money, fearing for our survival, and compromising ourselves for a sense of security. They help us see the reality our thoughts, feelings, and actions are creating, and they encourage us to shift our awareness around these situations and work toward manifesting something better. It's important to remember that nothing is set in stone—not even earthy Pentacles. Matter is just energy vibrating at a certain frequency. When we change that frequency to make it more harmonious and resonant with our spirit, the outer manifestations change for the better.

Take Stock

It might be a good idea to do some self-inquiry work to see where your predominant beliefs come from. Then you can begin clearing those that are no longer applicable or helpful. The more you can release limiting beliefs and open yourself to higher guidance, the more accurate your readings will become.

Change Your Mind

Because thoughts are ephemeral, they haven't solidified into feelings, actions, and manifestation yet and can be changed quickly. Think about it: you can swap a negative belief for a positive belief in an instant. Of course, establishing a new, habitual way of thinking will take a bit more time. But consistently focusing on positive thoughts can shift a deeply held negative belief. And Tarot can help you see where you need to do that. Once you understand the particular belief indicated by a card, you can create a positive affirmation or mantra to address it. (Or guide the person you're reading for to do so.) Change your mind, change your life!

Positive Cards

After all that focus on the so-called negative cards, let's look at the positive cards. This is much simpler because the positive cards are basically guideposts, letting you know you're on the right track. When they appear in a reading, they give you a lift. Depending on the card, they may confirm your own intuition about a particular situation or offer you hope for the future.

As always, the major arcana cards offer overarching guidance. For example, The Sun comes up in a spread to let you know that happier days are ahead. Positive cards in the minor arcana indicate resonance in a particular area. For example, the Eight of Wands represents freedom of movement; the Three of Cups signifies celebrating love; and the King of Pentacles promises financial security. And let's not forget the Ace of Swords: clear inspiration!

When someone we're reading for has a preponderance of positive cards, there's a good chance they need a boost. Maybe they've been going through a difficult time, and their confidence is waning. So they come to you, looking for guidance, and you get to be the bearer of good news. The cards encourage them to keep on keeping on.

Another common scenario is when a person who comes to a reading is considering a major change in their life. With the thought of any change, no matter how welcome it may be, comes fear. Human beings seem to be hardwired that way—to think *same* means *safe*, even when all the evidence in our lives points to the contrary. Tarot can be extremely helpful and clarifying in those moments. And when the layout of cards is full of positive guidance or indicates a positive outcome, it can give the querent the confidence to make that change.

The Magic of Tarot

Even if the person you're reading for is a huge skeptic—maybe they came to you for a reading to humor a friend—Tarot will affect them. There's simply something magical about a Tarot reading. A person shuffles this strange deck of cards and hands them to you. No one can see what they are because they're facedown. Then you take the top card off the deck one at a time and put them in a certain order. Suddenly there's a plethora of color, symbolism, and mystical imagery in front of this person. As you start validating things they've felt, are experiencing, and have been wondering about, something shifts in them. They walk away from the reading feeling seen and inspired. This is the true magic of Tarot! And even the most recalcitrant person can't help but feel touched by it.

The Timing of the Cards

Tarot is a tool we use to activate our intuition. The good news is that tapping into our intuition allows us to receive higher guidance. The bad news is that intuition operates outside of linear space and time, which makes ascribing timelines to the guidance difficult. But there are a few ways to put the cards' messages into the context of time.

Because major arcana cards represent archetypal, overarching themes, they indicate processes playing out over a longer time span. A general rule of thumb is that you'll see their guidance play out in six months to a year. Of course, that depends on where they show up in a spread (past, future, or central placement). In other words, if the major arcana card is in the past placement of a reading, that theme's influence is over. If it's the central message, you'll see its influence over the next six to twelve months. If it's in the future placement, the six-to-twelve-month process will begin in the future. So we look to the minor arcana to give us more specificity on timing. Here's a basic guideline on timing by suit:

Swords. The air element indicates the fastest timing because of the speed of thought. Although deeply held beliefs take time to change, an epiphany or "aha" moment happens instantaneously. You can quickly and easily recognize how any particular thought impacts you. And you can come up with a positive affirmation in its place in a few moments. So, generally speaking, Swords indicate a timeline of minutes or hours.

Cups. The water element usually takes a bit more time than air or fire because feelings and emotional states are weightier. You may understand intellectually that it's time to let something or someone go, for example, but your feelings have to catch up with

your thoughts before you can really do it. And that means taking the time to process and move through your emotions. Feeling our feelings isn't really encouraged in our culture. We have been taught to avoid sadness and grief. There is a superstition that if we really feel our feelings, we'll never move through them, when the opposite is true. Feelings are the realm of water, fluid and ready to move, so Cups often indicate a timeline of days.

Wands. The fire element typically indicates inspiration and motion. If you say that someone is "on fire," you mean that the person is full of passion and enthusiasm. Once a fire is lit, it naturally wants to burn. And the hotter a fire gets, the faster it burns. When you're clear on what you think and how you feel, then action naturally follows. And when you feel inspired, you move quickly. With that in mind, Wands often indicate a timeline of days to weeks.

Pentacles. The earth element indicates the slowest timing. This is the suit of money, physical growth, and manifestation—all of which take time. Think about a seed planted in the ground: It doesn't grow overnight. It needs time to absorb nutrients and water in the soil before building up the energy to burst through the crust of the earth and into the air. Then it needs sunlight and more water to grow from a seedling into a plant, which can take months. And if it's to grow into a tree, then full maturation takes much longer. I'm sure you'll get the metaphor here. The bigger the endeavor, the longer it takes to come to fruition. But Pentacles generally indicate a timeline of weeks to months.

Keeping Time in Perspective

Understanding these representations can be helpful, but the fact is that much of life's timing depends on us. Our expectations, choices, and actions (or lack thereof) can alter the events laid out in a reading. And being dead-set on a certain outcome that isn't in the cards for you will delay what is.

Let's say you have the Two of Cups in the near-future position in a reading. It feels like love is coming tomorrow! But you're sure that your crush is "the one" even though it's long past time to move on. Holding on to the wrong person will keep someone new from entering your life, pushing that card's promise further and further out. Your soulmate could be hovering around the periphery of your life, but you won't see them until you release your expectations.

The messages in Tarot are there to help if you're willing to let them. If the timing of a reading seems off, ask yourself this: are you trusting the Universe and going with the flow, or are you desperately hanging on to something? If you're clutching at a branch instead of flowing with the current, it will take longer to get to your destination. On the other hand, impatience indicates that you have more to understand in your current circumstance before change can occur.

Present Time

The concept of time is just that—a concept! There's nothing wrong with thinking about the past or the future unless you're letting the present moment pass you by. Your life is happening now. And you can only hear your intuition and receive guidance when you are present. So don't worry too much about timelines. Instead, use the cards' guidance to do what you can in this moment and create the life you want.

✳ READING FOR ANOTHER PERSON ✳

You've probably noticed how much easier it is to see another person's issues than your own. That's because you're seeing what's happening from an outside perspective. With this in mind, let's focus on reading for another person first. If you're a beginner, then tell your friends or colleagues you're learning Tarot and ask if you can practice on them. Most people will be happy to oblige.

How to Begin

Choose which spread you're going to use before you begin to lay out the cards so there's absolutely no confusion about the order in which you place the cards. This is when having practiced and memorized each spread and the meanings of every position can really come in handy. But if you're still finding your way, work with smaller spreads until you feel comfortable with each one. You may also choose a spread based on the querent's intention or question.

Begin every reading with your ritual: create a sacred space, connect to higher guidance, and breathe deeply, incorporating the other person into your ritual. See them connected, grounded, and protected. You can visualize them in a column of white light or just think the words "connect, ground, protect" with them in mind. Then reinforce this protection by asking that their intuition be heightened during the reading so they can receive helpful messages directly. (Refer to page 33 if you need a more detailed refresher.)

Next, ask the querent to set an intention for their reading. They can share this with you or not, depending on their preference. It may be easier to avoid discussing any details of what's going on for them before the reading. This allows you to just focus on the guidance that's coming through without getting into their story. As the reader, simply ask for the highest guidance to come through for them.

If the other person is physically present, then have them shuffle the deck (keeping the cards facedown). Make sure they shuffle enough to really move the cards around. This may sound rather magical, but shuffling gives their energy a chance to merge with the cards. You can think of this as activating the law of resonance or synchronicity. As they shuffle the deck, their life force aligns with the cards. When this process feels complete to them, have them use their left hand to cut the cards into three piles and then reassemble the deck into one pile in any order, still keeping the cards facedown.

Reading from a Distance

If this is a distance reading (meaning the other person is not sitting with you as you do the reading), then you will shuffle the cards for that person. Use the same protocol as you would if they were in the same room as you. Then, as you shuffle, set an intention for the highest guidance to come through the cards for them. When ready, complete the process by cutting the deck with your left hand and reassembling it into one pile in any order.

A Tarot reading for someone who is not physically present is just as effective as any other reading. You can work by phone or video call, and the process works the same way. Think of it this way: You're not connecting to the other person *physically* even if they're sitting right there with you. You are always connecting to Source energy to obtain guidance for them.

Bonus Cards

There are two extra cards that can find their way
into a reading. Sometimes, a card flies out of the
deck while someone shuffles. If this happens, take note of
the card but then have the person put it back in the deck and
continue shuffling. Also, the card at the bottom of the deck after
you have shuffled, cut the cards, and reassembled the deck reflects
the underlying message of the reading, an energy that's present
under the surface of your awareness. You can include the
messages of both of these cards in the reading if you like;
just think of them as addendums to the reading.

A Healing Practice

In many spiritual traditions, it's customary to dedicate a healing practice to the good of all. When you read for someone else with the intention of receiving the highest guidance to assist the other person, you elevate the reading into a healing practice. If this resonates with you, you can add this dedication to your ritual before beginning the reading.

Interpreting the Cards

Once the person you're reading for has finished shuffling the cards, cutting the deck, and putting the cards back into one pile, slowly and methodically take cards off the top of the pile and lay out your spread. Soften your gaze and begin to note your first impressions. Start tapping into your intuition and asking yourself questions about the cards and the guidance they offer.

Instead of just writing everything down like you do when reading for yourself, start talking! Don't analyze or edit yourself. Stay in a stream of consciousness and resist the urge of the logical left brain to immediately try and make sense of the spread. This isn't about you. Just focus on the cards, remembering to soften your gaze and tap into their energy.

Once you have the lay of the land, you can start sharing your interpretation of the cards' meanings and placements. Speak honestly about what you are perceiving. If no words are coming to you, ask yourself what you see, hear, and feel. Keep your attention on the spread of cards and not on the other person.

Staying Neutral

Although you're speaking to the other person, avoid looking at them and try to stay detached from their reactions. When reading for another person, you need to be very mindful of your facial expressions. Keep them neutral. Often, the person you're reading for is a little nervous. They're afraid of hearing something they won't like. And they're hoping to hear things that confirm and validate what they want. That's just human nature. But they're watching you for signals.

When you're reading, you're seen as being in a position of authority. Objectively, of course, this isn't true—you're simply the messenger. The guidance comes from Source energy or the other person's higher self, and it's being relayed to them by the cards. However, as the messenger—the interpreter of this symbolic language—you can certainly influence whether this is a positive, healing experience or not. So it's imperative that you don't color the experience with your own personal reactions. This goes back to the original intention: for the most helpful and highest guidance to come through you.

Answering Questions

Once you've done an overview of the reading and shared all the guidance that's come to you, then you can open the reading up for questions from the other person. They may ask for clarification about what you've shared. As they do, look to the positioning of the cards for answers. For example, if the questions have to do with the person's surroundings or other people in their life, look to the cards that address those things in the context of their placements. A reading has layers. You start with the story the spread tells, then you go into the specifics relayed by each card in each position. You'll find that the longer you stay with the cards, the more they will reveal.

Often what a person thinks is the main issue in their life, isn't. And the cards don't lie. For example, if a person is focused on practical matters, but there are a lot of Swords in their reading, the main areas in need of their attention are their mind, beliefs, and thinking patterns. This is where the person can achieve the greatest results. Of course, opening your mind and changing negative beliefs will impact practical matters, so their questions about practical matters will be answered—just not in the way they expect.

Here's another example: Say someone is coming to you with relationship questions. They're trying to figure out if the person they're interested in is "the one." In the reading, you will certainly be able to see if love is in the cards for them. If The Lovers or the Two of Cups turns up, a love relationship is indicated. But a person often comes to the table with a specific love interest in mind. The more deeply convinced they are that this person is their soulmate, the more you'll have your work cut out for you if the cards' guidance says otherwise. The best course is to encourage them to keep an open mind and allow the Universe to guide them. It always knows best. But if they're really entrenched, simply convey the information and leave it at that.

Remember, objectivity is crucial in all readings. When someone comes to you with an agenda (as they often do), you need to remain as removed from it as possible so you can give them helpful guidance. This is why detachment is so important. Focus on the cards in front of you and the multifaceted guidance they offer.

Avoid Repeat Readings

Be wary of someone coming to you frequently for readings. This can indicate that they're relying too heavily on your guidance and not trusting their own intuition. You don't want to enable a dependency. If you notice this happening, you can suggest that the other person get a Tarot deck and start strengthening their own guidance system.

You may also encounter people getting the same reading over and over—maybe not the exact cards in the same order, but the same themes repeating themselves. This happens when the person isn't working with the guidance you've already given them. You're simply the messenger, the person laying out the road map for them. They need to take the journey themselves. You have the option of declining readings for people when you see it's not really helping. But, typically, people will stop coming on their own if they feel the readings aren't helping them. And remember: this applies to you too. If you keep getting repeat messages in your readings, stop reading and start moving!

✳ READING FOR YOURSELF ✳

Doing a reading for yourself can be tricky because you're in the middle of your own life situations, which is to say that your experience will skew your perception. That makes it harder to see the big picture, distance yourself from your emotions and beliefs, and maintain objectivity. However, there are a few ways to mitigate this problem.

Reading for the Right Reasons

Starting with the right intention makes all the difference. When you approach a reading with the intention of seeking guidance rather than trying to predict the future, you establish a solid foundation to build on. Being open to guidance, to seeing beyond the analytical mind, creates the right conditions to receive that higher guidance. You can't use Tarot to try to control the narrative. And the more you override the temptation to use Tarot to try to manipulate a situation, the easier it becomes to stay open and hear what your higher self is trying to tell you.

Remember that trying to predict the exact way events will play out never works. The brain is like a computer: it can only process the data that's been put into it. In other words, we can only imagine what the future holds—and interpret the cards in future placements—based on our experience. But there are far more possibilities in life than we can imagine.

Reading for yourself allows you to explore your perspective, and that's very revealing in itself. A preponderance of one suit in a spread can show you what area of life you're focused on (or should be focusing on), whether it's your emotions (Cups), your mind (Swords), the actions you need to take (Wands), or your material life (Pentacles). And if there's a high percentage of major arcana cards, then you know big themes are at play.

Being open and receptive to any messages the cards reveal will enable you to see beyond your usual expectations. This is when you can see the big picture. If you approach the reading like a detective and follow the evidence, you'll arrive at conclusions that are unbiased and accurate.

Honor Your Ritual

Having a fruitful dialogue with your intuition means approaching readings for yourself in the same sacred manner as you do readings for others—taking the time to go through all the steps of your ritual. So always carve out a quiet place for yourself, connect to Source, take three deep breaths, and set an intention to receive the highest guidance. If you've added anything special to your ritual when doing readings for other people, such as lighting a candle or cleansing the space, then do that for yourself as well. Aren't you worth just as much care and attention as you give to others? When you begin readings from this calm, reverent place, you ensure a more powerful and helpful experience.

The Cards Aren't a Crutch

There's a belief in the Tarot world that it's dangerous to read for yourself too often. But it all depends on intention. If you're reading the cards all the time to predict how to handle daily situations, that's a rabbit hole you probably don't want to go down. The cards aren't magic; they are simply a reflection. If you're confused and tense and do readings for every little thing, you'll only become more confused and tense. Your perspective will narrow instead of broadening. Remember, it's important to come to each reading seeking the highest guidance, not a specific agenda.

Be Selective with Your Spread

It's important to choose a spread that matches the guidance you're seeking for yourself. A daily practice of one card is a wonderful way to develop a relationship with your inner guidance system. The three-card spread is good for a check-in or to gain a little more clarity around where you are.

Before embarking on the relationship spread, it's especially important to set the intention to understand the dynamics of your relationship with another person rather than asking a question that validates your desires or past perspective. With this spread, you really need to keep it clean—as in, not emotional, which can get messy. You may not get the message you're hoping for. The cards may even tell you to stop looking at the relationship dynamics with this person. It happens! If it happens to you, take a step back and enjoy the irony.

Save the more comprehensive V spread and Celtic Cross layouts for when you're ready to do a deep dive. It's best to have a clear head and as much detachment as you can muster before you begin these complex readings. That way, you can read all the layers of guidance offered by these spreads with the least amount of projection into the future as possible. If you come into the reading with fresh eyes, your intuition can guide you to the deeper meanings of the cards and their placements.

The Three-Times Rule

The Three-Times Rule refers to when a message finds its way to you three times. This could be something you see or hear in the world around you, or it could be a certain card coming up three times in a short time frame. When it happens, trust its guidance!

Be Mindful of Timing

There are no hard-and-fast rules regarding how frequently you should or should not do readings for yourself if you have the right intention. If you're a beginner, doing readings frequently can help you become more familiar with the process, and you'll be able to see overall patterns in your life. You may start to notice certain cards following you around. While this may be frustrating, it ensures that you get the intended message. The Universe is always speaking to us, and Tarot is a universal language. So if you have repetitive themes in the readings, pay attention to them.

Doing readings for yourself more often can also affect the timing of the guidance you receive. The more frequent your readings, the more immediate the guidance will be. That's because the messages in a reading are related to the events surrounding you at that particular time. For example, if you do a daily one-card reading, each day's reading will provide guidance for that particular day. A minor card would indicate focusing on that specific element (e.g., Swords = state of mind) for that day. A major card would indicate a broader theme, but it would still relate to the circumstances of that day. If you only come to Tarot occasionally to get a larger view of where you are, and you choose one of the more comprehensive layouts, your reading will follow the usual timeline guidance over a larger time frame.

Closing a Reading

Just as it is important to have a ritual to set up the reading, the same goes for closing the session. Whether you're reading in person, over a call, or for yourself, you want to cleanse the cards, clear your energy, and express gratitude for the guidance you've received. That way, you can keep your energy field clean and start fresh with every reading.

✳ CLEANSING THE CARDS ✳

Because the cards and the order they're in at the end of a reading reflect the guidance of that reading, you want to cleanse that energy from the deck after each one. You can do this by simply shuffling the cards. Think of a whiteboard in school: Once the lesson is over, the teacher erases the board. Otherwise, you would have layers of colorful writing, and the board would be an illegible mess. It's the same with Tarot, so shuffling is like erasing the board.

Another good maintenance practice is periodically cleansing the cards with sacred herbs or herbal incense, especially if you're doing a lot of readings for other people. You could also keep a quartz crystal with the cards. Add it to the bag in which you store the cards or lay it on top of the deck as part of your setup before a reading. Another thing you can do—and this may sound strange—is tap the deck with the side of your fist. This "pop" will clear the energy of the cards.

Intense Readings

If a session has been particularly intense or emotional for the other person, cleansing the area afterward will clear all the energy that was released. You can use any clearing technique that works for you, such as burning incense, visualizing white light, or using the sound of a bell or Tibetan singing bowl. This will dispel any thoughts, feelings, and speech from the reading and clear the space.

✳ CLEARING THE ENERGY ✳

Clearing your energy is extremely important when doing readings for other people. When you do a Tarot reading for someone, you're creating a sacred space with them. So when you're finished with the reading, you want to clear that space. This is easy to do: See the other person in the column of white light and set an intention that they are reinforced by Source energy. Then do the same for yourself. The column of light acts as a virtual waterfall of energy, cleansing any impressions you've received and reinforcing your energy field. We all have enough going on in our own energy fields, so there's no need to carry anyone else's stuff.

The same goes for readings for yourself. When you're finished with the reading, clear that energy out. This is especially important if you use the relationship spread and are actively connecting with the person you're in a relationship with. You want to keep your reading space clear and clean, but you also want to keep your own energy field clear and clean.

✳ CLOSING THE SPACE ✳

Once you've cleared the energy, say a quick prayer of gratitude or set an intention of closing the space. Saying a quick "thank you" to the Universe or to those angels and guides who've helped you receive the highest possible guidance never hurts. And marking the end of a reading helps you shift out of the mental state that you established during your pre-reading ritual and set healthy boundaries around your energy.

That's It!

Well, Tarot friends, that's the whole kit and kaboodle! You have all the tools you need to do a reading for yourself or another person. We've talked a lot about approaching a reading as a kind of spiritual practice, a process of self-inquiry or healing guidance. But don't let that become too heavy. Let it be spacious and light.

Have fun working with Tarot, and stay open to the possibilities it offers you. Like anything else, practice brings proficiency, and proficiency brings accuracy.

Refer back to the text when you need to, but keep moving forward in your journey. As long as you come to Tarot with the right intention and take the time to understand the cards and layouts, you'll be well on your way to a productive practice. And the process surrounding each reading will help you get there. Imagine you're the captain of a plane. You arrive at the airplane, do an inspection, and then get settled in the cockpit. You can use the following checklist to make sure you're ready to fire up the engine and prepare for takeoff. It's going to be a wonderful flight!

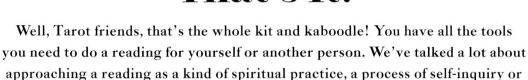

Your Reading Checklist

- ☐ Create a sacred space
- ☐ Connect, ground, and protect
- ☐ Take three deep breaths
- ☐ Set an intention
- ☐ Shuffle the cards
- ☐ Thoughtfully choose your spread
- ☐ Lay out the cards
- ☐ Take in the layout
- ☐ Note your intuitive impressions
- ☐ Note the meanings of cards and placements
- ☐ Interpret the guidance
- ☐ Clear the energy

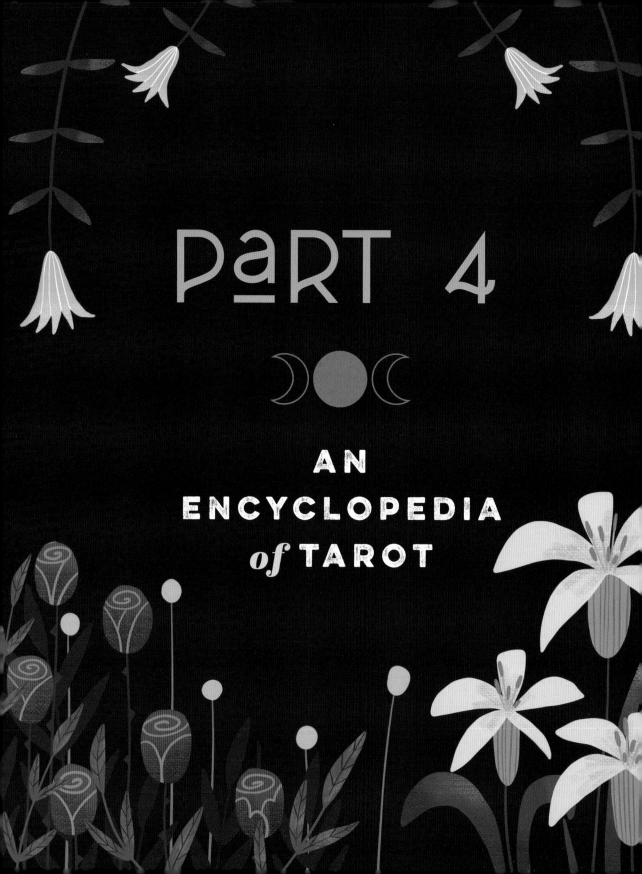

PART 4

AN ENCYCLOPEDIA *of* TAROT

Ace: The first card of each suit, the Ace bursts forth to awaken possibilities. The Ace represents powerful new beginnings and seed energy. Just as an acorn has all the potential of a fully grown oak tree, the Ace of each element carries all the potential of the fulfillment of the element. When an Ace presents itself, expect exciting new openings to occur:

- The Ace of Swords: new ideas, inspiration
- The Ace of Cups: new love, opening of the heart
- The Ace of Pentacles: new offers of money or material opportunity
- The Ace of Wands: new action

Air: The element of thought, the mind, mental states, and ideas. The suit of Swords represents the air element. When Swords shows up in a reading, it signifies what's going on in your head. Many of the Swords cards use negative imagery, representing worry, self-doubt, and psychological fear; however, inspiration, clear logic, and organized thinking are also represented in this suit.

Air signs: The astrological signs that correspond to the air element: Gemini, Libra, and Aquarius. Each of these signs has distinct qualities, but they're all predominantly governed by the mind. The court cards in the suit of Swords represent people and characteristics associated with the air signs. The Page of Swords, for example, signifies a person with an eager, restless mind who is always seeking to learn new things. (Any Gemini can relate to this!)

Aleister Crowley Tarot: The Tarot deck created by occult scholar Aleister Crowley and illustrated by Frieda Harris between 1938 and 1943. This deck wasn't published until 1969, years after their deaths. Crowley was a member of the Hermetic Order of the Golden Dawn, an English Rosicrucian society that brought the teachings of ancient Mystery Traditions into the modern era. He sought to update the symbolism of medieval classical Tarot.

Animal symbolism: The use of the qualities of animals as a guide for understanding our own nature or the time we're in. In Tarot, animals are often used to represent themes and guidance. For example, the lion in the major arcana card Strength (VIII) represents harmony with the power of our instinctual nature.

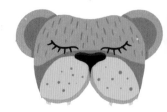

Aquarius: The eleventh sign of the zodiac, governing those born between January 20 and February 18. This air sign is represented by the constellation of Aquarius, the Water Bearer, and is ruled by Uranus. Those born under Aquarius have great mental aptitude, think outside the box, and are often quite brilliant as well as a bit eccentric.

Arcana: A noun derived from the Latin word *arcanus*, meaning "secrets or mysteries." It was used in English as the Dark Ages gave way to the Renaissance and there was a resurgence of Tarot in the general population. Arcana reflects a glimpse into the mysteries of the physical and spiritual worlds.

Archetype: A noun derived from the Greek *archein* (original) and *typos* (a model). Archetypes are symbols and personifications of energies that exist in the collective unconscious and are shared by all people, regardless of culture. Swiss psychiatrist and psychoanalyst Carl Jung popularized the concept to help identify recurring themes and motifs in a person's psyche. An example is the archetype of the hero, who's called to adventure and achievement. Understanding basic archetypes helps us interpret the themes of Tarot, especially of the major arcana.

Aries: The first sign of the zodiac, governing those born between March 21 and April 19. This fire sign is represented by the Aries constellation (aka the Ram) and ruled by Mars. Aries season begins on the spring equinox. Those born under this sign are strong, courageous pioneers who need to act on their impulses. Often uncomplicated, they move through their lives with bursts of energy.

Art: The expression of the Tarot motifs through drawings, paintings, and photographs; using the power of visual symbolism to ignite awareness in a nonlinear fashion.

Astrology: The study of the relationship between the stars and planets and man. Dating back 5,000 years, astrology was used by nearly every culture to calculate the cycles of the Earth and the solar system. The twelve signs of the zodiac provide a template for understanding an individual's personality.

B

Balance: An underlying theme in Tarot. The major arcana card Justice (XI) often depicts a woman holding a scale. This suggests a need to weigh options and find the correct action by balancing the qualities of giving and receiving, force and acceptance. The major arcana card Temperance (XIV) also touches on the theme of balance. We often perceive situations as either/or, or as a battle between the head and the heart. Temperance represents integrating the opposites, an alchemical process that brings wholeness—and the whole is worth more than the sum of its parts.

Beginner's mind: An approach to any subject or situation in which you keep an open mind, free from bias and fixed ideas. Bringing a beginner's mind to a Tarot reading helps you stay open to intuitive messages.

Belief system: The compilation of ideas and thought patterns a person has based on their socialization. This mental construct governs the way someone views themself and the world around them. It's a paradigm limited to the ego. Tarot can help you examine your belief system and how it affects your life, including bringing your attention to limiting beliefs so you can change them.

Breathwork: Breathing techniques that quiet the mind, increase energy, and activate the parasympathetic nervous system (to reduce stress and anxiety). Breathwork is often used in Tarot to clear your mind, connect with higher guidance, and tap into your intuition.

C

Cancer: The fourth sign of the zodiac, governing those born between June 21 and July 22. Cancer season begins on the summer solstice. This water sign is represented by the Cancer constellation, the Crab, and is ruled by the moon. Those born under this sign fit the archetype of the mother, nurturer, and protector and are emotional, sensitive, and often moody.

Capricorn: The tenth sign of the zodiac, governing those born between December 22 and January 19. Capricorn season begins on the winter solstice. This earth sign is represented by the Capricornus constellation (aka the Sea-Goat) and ruled by Saturn. Those born within this time frame are practical, grounded, traditional, and authoritative.

Cardinal signs: The four signs in astrology that begin on the cardinal celestial markers of the seasons: the spring and fall equinoxes, and the summer and winter solstices. They represent the powerful qualities of each season and are thus initiators of each element.

- Aries: fire
- Cancer: water
- Libra: air
- Capricorn: earth

Celtic Cross: The most classic and comprehensive Tarot spread, consisting of ten placements that show the energies around a person and the future trajectory they are on. This spread offers a wealth of information and a wide-angle view of a situation rather than focusing on a specific moment or question.

Chakra: "The wheel" in Sanskrit. One of seven energy centers in the body that correspond to certain nerves, organs, and functions. These centers need to remain open and aligned to promote health and vitality. The seven centers are:

- Root chakra: base of spine
- Sacral chakra: sexual organs
- Solar plexus chakra: stomach area
- Heart chakra: center of chest
- Throat chakra: throat and neck
- Third eye chakra: area slightly above and between the eyebrows
- Crown chakra: top of the head

Both Strength (VIII) and The Sun (XIX) in the major arcana carry the energy of the solar plexus chakra.

Chariot: A major arcana card (VII). The Chariot signifies preparation, planning, and getting ready to move forward. The Chariot is a vehicle that's ready for a journey. Imagine preparing for a road trip: getting the car fueled up, checking the tires, planning the route, consulting a map or GPS, packing, and organizing so that, when it's time to go, you are ready.

Charles VI deck: One of the oldest known Tarot decks (circa 1392), also called the Gringoneur deck after artist Jacquemin Gringoneur, who painted the commissioned deck.

Clairaudience: The extrasensory perception that refers to hearing what is inaudible. Clairaudience allows you to receive guidance intuitively of sounds, music, and words. You can develop and use this awareness when interpreting a reading.

Clairsentience: The extrasensory perception felt in the body through either emotions or subtle physical sensations. Clairsentience is often perceived as a gut feeling. Like clairaudience and clairvoyance, you can develop and use this awareness when interpreting a reading.

Clairvoyance: The extrasensory perception linked to vision, seeing beyond what can normally be perceived. Clairvoyance presents as seeing auras and energy or receiving intuitive visual impressions in the mind. This is what is commonly regarded as psychic vision.

Clearing energy: The practice of using herbs, incense, or white light to cleanse a person or space. When used before or after a reading, this helps dispel lingering

energy between the reader and the person being read, as well as from the room where the reading took place, so it doesn't affect those involved or future readings.

Collective unconscious: The universal field of consciousness common to all mankind from which archetypes, memories, and primordial images emerge. A theory of Carl Jung's, it explains why disparate cultures share similar stories. Understanding these common threads helps us interpret the symbolism in Tarot.

Coins: Another name for the suit of Pentacles in Tarot, which represents money, material objects, and physicality. In most Tarot decks, the pentacles themselves are depicted as discs with a pentagram or five-pointed star on them.

Colors: Used to convey esoteric symbolism in Tarot. Each color carries a meaning that can be used to deepen your interpretation of any card:

- Red: passion and authority
- Orange: vitality and creativity
- Yellow: optimism and power
- Green: health and growth
- Blue: peace and intuition
- Purple: enlightenment
- White: purity
- Black: the unknown potential
- Gray: mental activity
- Silver: clarity
- Gold: illumination

Completion: Coming full circle with conscious awareness. The concept of completion is represented by The World (XXI) in the major arcana. All aspects of a situation are in harmony for a successful conclusion, and they point to an imminent new beginning.

Conscious mind: The thought processes we're aware of. The Celtic Cross spread includes a placement that represents the conscious mind, indicating the reader's or querent's current awareness (i.e., where your or their head is at the present time).

Context: Pulling all the aspects of a Tarot reading together—including the meaning of each card, its placement, and its relationship to the other cards—to create a narrative. Understanding each card relative to the whole spread.

Core message: The main theme of a Tarot card, or the central card in a layout. In a multi-card reading, the card in this placement offers the context in which the other cards should be read.

Court cards: The four cards in each suit that, when they appear in a reading, represent other people in a person's life or personality traits in an individual. The page is youthful, the knight is dynamic, the queen is the feminine aspect of the suit, and the king is the masculine aspect of the suit. Each court card has characteristics that correspond to astrological signs, and every person can find their sign or basic nature represented in a court card. It's important to remember that court cards in a person's reading can indicate a characteristic that the person is embodying just temporarily. For example, a King of Wands in a young woman's reading is guiding her to harness her own masculine energy and focus on accomplishing her goals.

Crown: A symbol that represents spiritual enlightenment and sovereignty. The Emperor (IV) and The Empress (III) in the major arcana are usually portrayed wearing crowns, signifying that they are masters of their realms.

Crystals: Semiprecious stones and minerals used to cleanse, heal, and align energy. For example, keeping a quartz crystal with your Tarot deck will help clear the energy of the cards. This is especially necessary if numerous people are shuffling the deck.

Cups: A suit in the minor arcana that represents water, which is the element of feeling, emotion, sensitivity, relationships, and love in all its forms: romantic, familial, self-love, and spiritual love. It is also the conductor of intuition. We need sensitivity to understand our own feelings and those of others.

Cutting the deck: The final step in shuffling the Tarot cards for a reading. In card games, cutting the deck means splitting it into two or more piles placed next to each other. In Tarot, it means using the left hand to make three piles of cards. You'll then reassemble the deck in any order while keeping the cards facedown, also using your left hand.

Dark: The unknown, the area of life not seen. Also, one of a pair of opposites: light and dark. Note that the dark is not inherently scary or evil but rather in need of illumination. The expression "I'm in the dark" points to this.

Death: A major arcana card (XIII) of transformation. The Death card is *not* a signifier of physical death. It is symbolic. But it's an indicator of profound change. Some aspect of our life (which will be indicated by the surrounding cards) is over. This could refer to a job, a residence, or a way of being in the world. With death comes rebirth. One door is closing so another may open.

Deck: The whole of the Tarot (seventy-eight cards) or any pack of cards, including but not limited to Tarot, playing cards, or oracle cards.

Detachment: The conscious state of separating from a situation to understand it better. Detaching helps you gain objectivity and an understanding of the big picture in Tarot. It allows you to see the forest for the trees

Devil: A major arcana card (XV) indicating the need to let go. The Devil is probably the most misunderstood card in all of Tarot. It symbolizes entrapment, being caught in social conditioning, or feeling that someone is not free to be themselves. This card is a call for liberation. It represents an opportunity to free yourself from superstition. Trust your instincts, not the collective fear around you.

Divine: A term pointing to the spiritual world and its influence on the material world, such as *divine intervention*. Used synonymously with Source energy and grace as "the Divine" under the belief that a higher power will guide you. In numerology, the number zero represents the Divine and brings blessings to whatever number it accompanies.

Earth: The element signifying money, material reality, stability, and the realm of the physical. The suit of Pentacles (also known as *Coins*) represents the earth element. When Pentacles show up in a reading, it signals that the material aspects of your life are key at this time. This could indicate a need to focus on financial issues or material security, or on your health and well-being. It's also a call to remember that the earth element is just one of four elements, which all coexist together and affect each other.

Earth signs: The astrological signs of Taurus, Virgo, and Capricorn. Each of these signs is related to the earth-element themes of physicality, sustenance, and the material world. The court cards of the suit of Pentacles correspond to people born under the earth signs or an aspect of yourself related to the material or physical realm. For example, the Queen of Pentacles signifies a time to nurture yourself.

Egypt (Ancient): A highly evolved ancient civilization where some believe Tarot originated. Egypt had its own symbolic language (hieroglyphics) and was home to the Mystery Schools, which date back to 1500 BC and shared ancient esoteric knowledge.

Eight: A number that represents strength, success, growth, ambition, and courage. Strength (VIII) carries the energy of the number eight.

Eighteen: A sacred number reduced to nine (one plus eight) in numerology. It represents new life. In the major arcana, The Moon (XVIII) carries the energy of the number eighteen.

Element: A term used in Tarot and astrology to denote the four types of energy: fire, earth, air, and water are the elements that make up the terrestrial world.

Eleven: A powerful Master Number in numerology that signifies the power of the spirit. Also known as the Master Intuitive, eleven represents inspiration, vision, and spirituality. In relationships, it demands independence and self-actualization from both parties. In the major arcana, Justice (XI) carries the energy of the number eleven.

Emperor: A major arcana card (IV) that represents the fully actualized masculine principles of leadership, entrepreneurship, great capabilities, manifestation, and authority. It is a card of sensible action characterized by the builder, who is grounded, strong, and confident. It tells you not to be afraid to go out into the world and make things happen.

Empress: A major arcana card (III) that signifies the fully actualized feminine energies of abundance, beauty, fecundity, and creativity. The empress is usually portrayed as a full-bodied woman surrounded by the fruits and flowers of the earth. Her energy is regal, confident, and a good sign of fertility on all levels, including in business, beautifying the home, and possibly motherhood.

Energy: The underlying substance of all matter. Everything is energy vibrating at a certain frequency. Energy can also refer to the intuitive sense or feeling you get from something or someone, as in "this space has good energy." It can also refer to the meaning behind something, such as a symbol on a Tarot card. The archetypes, suits, symbols, and numbers of the major and minor arcana all carry their own unique energy. Combined in a reading, those energies can provide you with meaning and guidance.

Energy field: A term in metaphysics used to identify the auric field around a person, place, or thing.

Epiphany: An "aha" moment when you suddenly understand something at a deep level. This happens often in Tarot as you gain a deeper awareness of yourself and your life.

Extrasensory perception (ESP): Also called the sixth sense, this is the ability to perceive beyond the five senses and tune into the subtle senses. Clairvoyance, clairaudience, and clairsentience are all aspects of ESP.

Extrovert: A person with more dynamic energy that needs to be expressed outwardly. This energy is represented in Tarot by the suit of Wands, which embodies the realm of activity and movement.

Feminine: An expression not limited to the female sex; energy that is receptive, nurturing, intuitive, and feeling in nature. The yin aspect.

Fifteen: A number that carries the energy of freedom and individuality regarding personal responsibilities. In numerology, fifteen is reduced to six (one plus five), which essentially signifies the emancipation of the feminine. In the major arcana, The Devil (XV) carries the energy of the number fifteen.

Fire: The element signifying action, enthusiasm, and movement. Fire is represented in Tarot by the suit of Wands, which indicates the need to focus, move, or moderate your energy. In a reading, the Wands' guidance suggests moving with awareness and clarity.

Fire signs: The astrological signs Aries, Leo, and Sagittarius. These signs have the element of fire in common: Aries represents the new spark and a call to purposeful action, Leo prizes self-expression and sharing, and Sagittarius is  the adventurer. The court cards of Wands correspond with people born under these signs or with an aspect of yourself. For example, the Queen of Wands is an extroverted woman who is generous with those around her.

Five: A number signifying restless energy, communication, and the need to act on desires. In the major arcana, The Hierophant (V) carries the energy of the number five.

Fixed signs: The four astrological signs of Taurus, Scorpio, Aquarius, and Leo. These signs stabilize their elements of earth, water, air, and fire, respectively. Those born under the fixed signs are more grounded in their element. Fixed signs fall at the midpoints of each season, when that season is the most rooted.

- Taurus: mid-spring
- Scorpio: mid-fall
- Aquarius: mid-winter
- Leo: mid-summer

Flemish Hunting Deck: A set of fifty-two cards created around the year 1480. Also known as the Cloisters Playing Cards, this deck is believed to be one of the earliest examples of a Tarot deck being converted into modern playing cards. The only known complete deck of these playing cards is from the fifteenth century and is on display at the Metropolitan Museum of Art in New York City.

Fool: The first card of the major arcana (0). The Fool signifies the need to have total trust in the Divine and begin a grand new adventure. This card is a powerful indicator to follow your heart.

Four: The number representing practicality, stability, and prudence. It's associated with the earth element and can indicate that someone is careful, conservative, and prone to rigidity. It carries a masculine energy. In the major arcana, The Emperor (IV) carries the energy of the number four.

Fourteen: A number that indicates the balance between stability and activity. In numerology, it's reduced to five (one plus four). This number indicates the integration of something new to enlarge your world. In the major arcana, Temperance (XIV) carries the energy of the number fourteen.

G

Gemini: The third sign of the zodiac, governing those born between May 21 and June 20. Gemini is ruled by the planet Mercury and represented by the Gemini constellation (aka the Twins). Those born under this air sign are quick thinking and curious, and they need constant mental stimulation. Playful communication is a hallmark of this sign. The court cards of Swords can signify a Gemini person or those exemplifying the sign's characteristics.

God/Goddess: A personification of divine Source energy in various cultures. Gods represent the various aspects of the divine masculine, and goddesses embody various traits of the divine feminine. For example, the Greek goddess Aphrodite (or Venus in Roman mythology) is the well-known goddess of love, sensuality, romance. Her energy can be found in the major arcana card The Empress (III).

Grace: A state of ease, wonder, and peace. An unexpected blessing or divine intervention.

Grail: A chalice or cup. The suit of Cups in classical Tarot uses the imagery of the grail to signify a vessel carrying emotions. In many decks, the Ace of Cups portrays a grail overflowing with universal love.

Guidance: Direction from a figure of authority or an inspired source. We use Tarot and other divination tools to obtain divine or energetic guidance that reaches beyond our own experience and to seek higher awareness of ourselves or any situation we are in.

Hanged Man: A major arcana card (XII) that often portrays a man hanging upside down from a tree. It symbolizes the need to totally let go, to surrender your agenda to a higher power, and to be open to what happens next. Consciously choosing to release your perspective or attachment to an outcome will facilitate a needed new perspective.

Hermit: A major arcana card (IX) representing walking the spiritual path. The Hermit is usually portrayed as an older wise man carrying a lantern and walking stick. This card signifies navigating a path less traveled using your own light (your inner guidance system, or intuition). This is a card of great autonomy, encouraging you to embrace your uniqueness.

Hierophant: A major arcana card (V) signifying spiritual authority. The Hierophant is usually portrayed as a high priest or pope. In a reading, this card can point to meeting a spiritual teacher or encountering a body of teachings. An old-fashioned interpretation of this card is an upcoming marriage. The Hierophant card symbolizes bringing light into darkness and a time of spiritual awakening in the world.

High Priestess: A major arcana card (II) representing powerful intuitive abilities. The High Priestess symbolizes the deep, mysterious, secretive aspects of the feminine. This card signifies a time to access your inner guidance system, to detach from the conventional ideas of the world, and to seek the counsel of your own oracle. It tells you that you can have emotional balance, independence, and trust in yourself.

Hit: A colloquialism used to mean a strong intuitive feeling. You might say you got a hit off a particular card to indicate that you have an innate understanding of it or feeling about it.

I

I: The Roman numeral for the number one, used throughout the major arcana.

Iconography: Images or symbols used to convey spiritual teachings; artwork that awakens the senses to the mystical realms. Tarot decks are filled with widely varying iconography to help deliver their guidance.

Imagery: Illustrations used in Tarot to convey mystical knowledge to the reader. This visual medium transcends the linear logical mind, bringing a greater depth of information to the observer.

Impressions: Personal interpretations of and intuitive feelings about Tarot cards during a reading. Focusing on what you feel, see, and hear will activate your intuitive guidance and allow you to receive impressions. Trust them without overanalyzing the information they offer.

Integration: The process of merging various themes and ideas to achieve a cohesive whole, including the blending of opposites. In Tarot, you integrate the numerous cards and their placements in a reading to interpret the overall guidance.

Intention: A clear objective. The act of setting an intention directs your energy and actions. In Tarot, always come to a reading with the intention of receiving the highest guidance in addition to any specific intention. In life, remember that a positive intention will produce positive results while a negative or calculating intention will ultimately create chaos and negative results.

Interpretation: An understanding or explanation of something, including a Tarot card or spread, that varies from person to person. You'll find numerous Tarot guidebooks in stores, online, and with decks, and their interpretations of the card meanings can vary widely. While referring to guidebooks is necessary when learning Tarot, your own intuitive understanding of the cards will ultimately offer the most accurate interpretation. After all, when you're the reader, the guidance is coming through you.

Introvert: A person with a quieter, introspective energy who often needs to withdraw and process information internally. This energy is represented in Tarot by the suit of Swords, which embodies the realm of thought.

Intuition: The ability to understand something without using logical, analytical reasoning; an instantaneous knowing or gut feeling. It may take the form of visual, auditory, or physical sensations.

We are always receiving intuitive information, but, for most people, it's drowned out by the chatter of the mind. Meditation and various techniques to quiet the mind are essential for accessing intuition. Tarot cards help strengthen your intuition through their use of archetypal images, symbols, and colors.

Jack: A face card in modern playing cards, equivalent to the page and knight court cards in Tarot. If reading with regular playing cards, a jack represents a blend of the youthful qualities of a page and the dynamic energy of a knight.

Journey: A story told by Tarot cards. In a reading, a spread of cards outlines the person's journey from where they've come from to where they are headed. This term also applies to the progress of the major arcana cards, beginning with The Fool (0) and ending with The World (XXI).

Judgment: The major arcana card (XX) representing a state of much greater awareness, discernment, and good choices. This card indicates that objectivity and a higher perspective are available to you. You can rise from a very limited personal perspective to understand the collective—in other words, go beyond the confines of your egoic mind.

Jupiter: The fifth planet from the Sun and the largest planet in our solar system, with an orbital period of twelve years. Also, the Roman name for the Greek god Zeus. This planet rules the zodiac sign of Sagittarius and represents growth, great expansion, and opportunity. Its placement in an astrological birth chart indicates the area of life that will bring good fortune. When Jupiter is in conjunction with another planet in a birth chart, it greatly amplifies the energy of that planet.

Justice: A major arcana card (XI) that signifies balance, weighing options, and thinking things through. In a reading, this card points to a time to detach emotionally and use the intellect to get clear and make a good decision. Justice is often portrayed as a woman holding scales in one hand and an upright sword in the other. This imagery offers a message to find balance rather than going to any extreme.

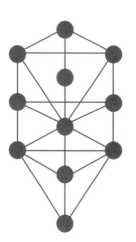

Kabbalah: Mystical Judaism; ancient esoteric teachings about the nature of reality. Kabbalah numerology is the predecessor of the modern Western, or Pythagorean, numerology used more widely today.

Key card: The card that holds the core message in a reading. Symbolically, it unlocks the guidance in a spread of cards. This card often sits in the outcome placement in layouts.

King: A court card in the four suits of the minor arcana. The king is the last card of each suit, signifying the full embodiment and masculine expression of the element of that suit:

- King of Swords: discipline and organized thinking, authority
- King of Cups: mastery of emotions, maturity
- King of Pentacles: great ability in the material realm, prosperity, security
- King of Wands: control and good use of your life-force energy

Knight: A court card in the four suits of the minor arcana. Knights represent dynamic movement in each element and a thirst for action regarding the particular suit:

- Knight of Swords: combative mental energy
- Knight of Cups: inspiration to act on strong feelings of love
- Knight of Pentacles: steady progress with a project
- Knight of Wands: going very rapidly toward a goal

Layout: Another term for a spread; the placement of Tarot cards that give structure to a reading. Laying out the cards in a particular order and in a variety of placements allows you to obtain different levels and degrees of insight and messages.

Left brain: The rational, logical, analytical mind. The left brain is associated with the right side of the body and the masculine qualities of thinking and judgment. It's often given precedence over the creative right brain in Western society, which can result in its being overactive.

Left side: In a Tarot spread, the cards to the left side of the central card represent the past. The left side of the body is associated with the feminine aspects of consciousness and is connected to the right brain—intuition, creativity, and spatial awareness.

Leo: The fifth sign of the zodiac, Leo is a fire sign. Ruled by the sun and represented by the Leo (or Lion) constellation, it governs those born between July 23 and August 22. Leos are charismatic, natural leaders with a creative flair for self-expression. In the northern hemisphere, Leo season is at the height of summertime, when having fun, playing, connecting with others, and enjoying life are emphasized.

Libra: The seventh sign of the zodiac. Ruled by Venus, this air sign governs those born between September 23 and October 22 and is represented by the Libra constellation (aka the Scales). Libra season begins on the autumnal equinox and is associated with the themes of balance, harmony, and relationships. People born during this time are conflict averse and weigh out every decision. Diplomacy and win-win solutions are hallmarks of this energy.

Light: All that is illuminated and understood. Also, one of the pair of opposites: light and dark. When written with a capital L, Light refers to Source energy.

Lovers: A major arcana card (VI). This card signifies romance, love relationships, partnerships, and sexuality. The Lovers are usually portrayed as a man and woman standing together in a garden, referencing the archetypes of Adam and Eve. When this card comes up in a reading, you can expect big themes of love and relationships in your life.

Magician: A major arcana card (I). The Magician is the link between Heaven and Earth, the spiritual and material worlds. He receives higher guidance, which he puts to use in his life. If this card comes up in a reading, it signifies that communication, grounding inspiration, and actualization are themes present in your life. It's time to channel those ideas into reality.

Mamluk deck: A deck of ornate, hand-painted cards thought to originate in the fifteenth century. They are named after the Mamluk Sultanate in Egypt and were brought to Europe sometime during the Islamic conquest. You can find artistic reproductions of the Mamluk deck in the Topkapi Museum in Turkey.

Mantra: A word or sound repeated to focus the mind and bring you into a higher state of consciousness. The concept originated in the ancient Hindu tradition. A modern adaptation of the mantra is any word or phrase you use repeatedly to focus your attention on what you want.

Mars: The fourth planet from the Sun with an orbital period of 687 days. Mars rules the astrological sign of Aries and is associated with the masculine energies of action, strength, and dynamic movement. Named after the god of war, it can indicate conflict in an astrological chart but is best understood as the warrior archetype, seeking to bring righteous action and justice.

Marseilles deck: One of the oldest known Tarot decks. Although it's thought to have originated in Milan in the fifteenth century, this deck was very popular in France in the seventeenth and eighteenth centuries and is still produced today. It is the oldest deck in continued use.

Masculine: An expression not limited to the male sex; used to describe energy that is rational, action oriented, and focused. The yang principle.

Meaning: The intention or message behind something. In Tarot, it refers to the definitions of cards and their placements and relates to the search for the inherent message of any card.

Meditation: The act of quieting the mind using breath, a mantra, or controlled movement practices such as yoga and tai chi to achieve focused consciousness. Meditation can help you strengthen your intuition and connection to Source, thereby enriching your Tarot practice.

Mercury: The closest planet to the Sun, making it the fastest planet in our solar system, with an orbital period of eighty-eight days. In astrology, this planet rules the signs of Gemini and Virgo and represents all forms of communication, messages, mental activity, and travel over short distances. Named for the god of communication and swiftness, Mercury is known as "the trickster" and indicates playful use of the intellect in the exchange of ideas. The Magician (I) in the major arcana is often portrayed as Mercury (Roman) or Hermes (Greek).

Message: Information and guidance obtained through Tarot about ourselves or any situation we're in. All the symbolism, colors, archetypes, and numbers in the seventy-eight cards of Tarot contain inherent messages for the reader.

Metaphor: A figure of speech using a word or phrase that is symbolic; a phrase that conveys an abstract concept. Often, intuition comes to us in the form of metaphors or symbols to illustrate a message with a deeper meaning.

Metaphysical: A noun derived from the Greek *meta ta physika* (meaning "after the things of nature") to describe the realm of reality that is beyond the five senses. It refers to the interplay of spiritual and philosophical themes in our lives and the understanding of the nature of reality beyond the mundane or physical world.

Moon: In astrology, the moon signifies our emotional, instinctual nature and the subconscious forces that motivate our behavior and reactions. The moon rules the sign of Cancer. It is a luminary representing the feminine energies of intuition and emotion that affect the water in our bodies, the growth of plants, and the tides. Its energy can be found in the major arcana's The High Priestess (II) and The Moon (XVIII), the latter of which indicates a need to stay very present so you can choose a new path and avoid falling back into unconscious patterns. In many ways, The Moon is a card of warning—don't look back! Instead, look toward the future and keep going.

Mundane: Referring to the normal sense perceptions of physical reality; a term used to signify the relative experiences of daily life. When you learn to look past the mundane, you can see the energetic or metaphysical reality pervasive within all physical phenomena.

Mutable signs: The four signs in astrology who fall at the end of each season: Gemini, Virgo, Sagittarius, and Pisces. These signs are changeable and adaptable but can also be more unstable. Those born under these signs are more fluid in their respective elements:

- Gemini: air
- Virgo: earth
- Sagittarius: fire
- Pisces: water

Mystery Schools: Ancient schools of esoteric teachings learned in secrecy. In numerous cultures, esoteric teachings were only available to carefully chosen initiates. These schools were kept out of plain sight to protect the powerful, sacred nature of the information that was passed down (usually orally) from teacher to student. Modern Mystery Schools, such as the Order of the Golden Dawn, have sought to preserve and update ancient esoteric knowledge and make it available to all who seek it.

N

Negative: Characterized by absence rather than presence. One of a pair of opposites, negative and positive, the term is often associated with the dark, receptive, or feminine aspects of energy. Seemingly negative cards and interpretations in a reading can often be the most helpful because they give you the opportunity to change what you don't like.

Neptune: The eighth and outermost planet from the sun with an orbital period of 165 years. Neptune was discovered in 1846 and named for the Roman god of the sea because of its watery blue color. In astrology, it represents intuition, dreams, and the collective unconscious. In a birth chart, it indicates that individual's spiritual awakening. Neptune rules the zodiac sign of Pisces.

Nine: The last base number in numerology. It represents completion, perfection, and wisdom as well as maturation and exaltation. Nine raises the vibration of any number it's added to. For example, three plus nine equals twelve, which is then reduced back to three but now also carries the energy of the numbers one and two. In the major arcana, The Hermit (IX) carries the energy of the number nine.

Nineteen: A number reduced to one (one plus nine, then one plus zero) in numerology. This number represents both beginning and completion, which makes for a favorable new start. In the major arcana, The Sun (XIX) carries the energy of the number nineteen.

19

Numbers: Another facet of Tarot's symbolism. In Tarot, you work with the energy of each number to obtain awareness of the underlying principles in a particular card of the major or minor arcana.

Numerology: The esoteric science of numbers. This ancient practice involves converting any letter to a numeric value to understand the energy of a name or word using the integers one through nine, as well as Master Numbers such as eleven and twenty-two, which each hold a particular significance. Numbers greater than nine are reduced by adding the digits until you have a single number and can discern its energy.

0

One: A number signifying initiation, new beginnings, and individuality. In the minor arcana of Tarot, the Ace of each suit is number one. In the major arcana, The Magician (I) carries the energy of the number one.

One-card spread: A simple layout that allows a reader to receive guidance about a central theme. This is a good practice to use for a daily meditation (setting an intention for the day), to learn Tarot, or to obtain a quick answer to a specific question.

Oracle: In ancient times, a seer or prophet/prophetess who could receive messages and guidance when in a trance or meditative state. Today, a metaphysical tool such as Tarot that acts as a mediator to help you understand the energy of any situation, as in consulting an oracle deck to access your intuition and receive guidance.

Osho Zen Tarot: A popular modern version of Tarot with an Eastern, philosophical approach to the card meanings. The information in its guidebook is based on the wisdom of the spiritual teacher Osho.

Outcome: The core message in a Tarot spread. The outcome card summarizes the advice in the reading and shows the results of the current trajectory of the person being read.

P

Page: The first of the four court cards in each suit of the minor arcana. The page signifies a child or young person with the qualities of their suit's element, or any person who has an open, playful energy for a period of time. By suit:

- Page of Swords: curious and inquisitive
- Page of Cups: emotionally open, trusts their heart
- Page of Pentacles: beginning a course of study or new project
- Page of Wands: playful, creative expression

Paradigm: A somewhat fixed system of thoughts, beliefs, or ideas that governs a person's perspective of themselves and their experiences. Working with Tarot helps you understand the paradigm you're in by reflecting through images and symbolism your belief system and behaviors so you can see how they're affecting your life more clearly.

Pattern: Anything that repeats in a systematic way. The world is built upon patterns of energy that consistently produce similar results, such as fractal shapes being repeated in nature. Recognizing patterns in your own life helps bring awareness to your core beliefs so you can bring about growth and positive change. When working with the Tarot repeatedly, you will also see patterns in the symbolism and inherent messages that help guide you.

Pentacles: A suit in the minor arcana that represents earth, which is the element of physicality and the material aspects of life: money, health, growth, and endeavors you wish to manifest.

Perception: The way you see yourself and others; the awareness you bring into any situation. Tarot helps you see what is possible beyond your senses' perception of reality.

Perspective: Your angle of awareness pertaining to anything or anyone; a point of view. Remember, there is more than one perspective. Using Tarot helps you see beyond your own perspective and gain a wider view of where you are in life and what is influencing you.

Pisces: The twelfth and final sign of the zodiac, governing those born between February 19 and March 20. Pisces is a water sign ruled by the planet Neptune and represented by the constellation of Pisces (the Fishes). This sign is associated with compassion and brotherly love, and those born under it are highly sensitive, imaginative, intuitive, and caring.

Placement: The specific position of a card within a Tarot layout, as in the ten placements of the Celtic Cross spread. Each placement in a spread has a particular significance. The placements give your reading context, allowing you to see how the cards relate to each other and your intention.

Pluto: Formerly the ninth planet from the sun in our solar system. It was discovered in 1930 and named for the god of the underworld in Roman mythology. Although Pluto was redefined as a dwarf planet in 2006, it's considered the most powerful planet in astrology. Pluto rules the zodiac sign of Scorpio and carries the energy of death, rebirth, sexuality, and pure life force. With an orbital period of 248 years, Pluto transits (when a planet moves across other planets in your chart) are rare and have a powerful effect in your life.

Position: Another word for placement, meaning where each card falls in a Tarot layout. The meaning of each card needs to be understood relative to its position (e.g., the past or the future placement) to obtain accurate guidance.

Positive: Characterized by presence rather than absence. One of the pair of opposites, positive and negative, the term is associated with masculine, outgoing, assertive energy. Positive cards in a reading tell you that you're on the right track.

Priest/Priestess: An individual devoted to the spiritual life who guides or performs sacred rites. Represented in the major arcana of Tarot by The High Priestess (II) and The Hierophant (V), these archetypes tell you to seek out the Divine in yourself and others.

Projection: The act of seeing another's behavior subjectively through your perspective and experience. When you project, you put your thoughts and feelings onto another person rather than observing that person clearly for who they are. In a reading, projection can muddle the cards' guidance and affect the accuracy of your interpretations. Bring your awareness back to your intuition to gain clarity.

Psychic: A term that loosely describes clairvoyance and mediumship. A psychic has heightened intuitive abilities and is able to perceive beyond the five senses. They have learned to tap into their intuition and understand the subtle senses.

Q

Queen: The feminine aspect of the court cards. The queen of each suit represents someone—often a woman—with the qualities of that suit's element, or guidance about energies someone will embody temporarily. The expressions of the queen in each suit are:

- Queen of Swords: stern and emotionally distant
- Queen of Cups: loving and receptive
- Queen of Pentacles: wealthy and sensual
- Queen of Wands: warm and sharing

Querent: The questioner in a Tarot reading. This can refer to the person you are reading for or to you if you are doing a reading for yourself.

Question: A specific topic that you (or the person you are reading for) are searching for guidance about. This can also be referred to as an intention. Our questions are often answered in unexpected ways, so coming to a Tarot reading with an open mind will enable you to receive the inherent guidance about your question.

R.

Reader: The person doing the Tarot reading. Whether you're reading for yourself or others, you are acting as an intermediary for higher guidance. This requires you to be objective and clear about what information you are seeking. Establishing a ritual to quiet your mind before a reading can help you access your intuition and interpret the guidance you receive.

Reading: The process of interpreting the symbolism, imagery, and numbers of Tarot cards in the context of your intention, the positions of the cards, and the cards' relationship to each other to understand the story they tell.

Relationship spread: The four-card spread used when seeking guidance about a relationship with another person. This layout is especially useful for understanding what you and the other person bring to the relationship and how that affects the relationship.

Renaissance: A period in Europe spanning from the late Middle Ages to the Age of Enlightenment (the fourteenth to seventeenth centuries). The Renaissance was a revival of humanism and a time of artistic proliferation. Tarot became very popular during this era.

Rider-Waite deck: The most well-known and commonly used Tarot deck, created by academic and mystic Arthur Edward Waite and drawn by Pamela Colman Smith. Both were members of the Hermetic Order of the Golden Dawn, a modern Mystery School. This deck was first published in 1909 by the Rider Company. Its medieval imagery is derived from early classic European decks.

Right brain: The side of the brain associated with the left side of the body and connected to the feminine qualities of intuition, imagery, and creativity. Quieting

the logical, analytical left brain allows access to the right brain and its intuition.

Right side: In a Tarot spread, the cards to the right of the central card relate to the future. The right side of the body is associated with the masculine, forward-moving, assertive aspects of consciousness.

Roman numerals: A number system from ancient Rome used in Europe well into the late Middle Ages. The twenty-two cards of the major arcana use Roman numerals that come from the Latin alphabet—I (one), V (five), and X (ten) are used in various combinations. The smaller number *before* the larger number subtracts from it (e.g., IV is the number four) and the smaller number *after* the larger number adds to it (e.g., VI is the number six).

Romani people: A nomadic people thought to have originated in Egypt. Many Romani people practice divination using Tarot or playing cards (the modern version of the minor arcana). The Romani culture, which is steeped in mysticism and music, is still widely present across Europe.

Ruling planet: The planet associated with a particular zodiac sign. Every astrological sign is governed by a ruling planet, a term used loosely to also include the Sun (ruler of Leo) and the Moon (ruler of Cancer). Ancient astrologers were astronomers, so they only used the planets visible to them (Mercury, Venus, Mars, Jupiter, and Saturn) as well as the Sun and Moon. Vedic astrology from India still uses only these ancient rulers. Modern astrology includes the planets Uranus, Neptune, and Pluto, which were discovered by astronomers starting in the late 1700s, perhaps giving more variety and insight into our relationship with our solar system in modern times.

Sacred space: A designated room or area for working with Tarot. Creating a sacred space by choosing a quiet space, lighting a candle, and cleansing the area signals your mind to shift and allow access to your intuition.

Sagittarius: The ninth sign of the zodiac, governing those born between November 22 and December 21. This fire sign is ruled by Jupiter and is associated with the Sagittarius (Archer) constellation. Those born under Sagittarius feel a need for movement and travel, and they always have a goal they're striving to achieve. Typically a positive, optimistic presence, a Sagittarian is at their best when they are focused on a spiritual quest.

Saturn: The sixth planet from the Sun, with an orbital period of twenty-nine years. Named after Saturnus, the Roman god of time and agriculture (Greek: Kronos), Saturn carries a powerful energy of focus and discipline. In astrology, it's the ruling planet of Capricorn. When Saturn appears in your birth chart, it shows the way to build a strong foundation for yourself. Saturn transits are good times in your life to be sober and practical and work on what needs to get done.

Scorpio: The eighth sign of the zodiac, governing those born between October 23 and November 22. This water sign is ruled by Pluto and is, in many ways, the most powerful sign in astrology. The themes of Scorpio are death, resurrection, and empowerment. Scorpio natives are highly sensitive but stable and self-protective. The Scorpius (Scorpion) constellation is associated with this sign, but the Eagle and Phoenix are also symbols of Scorpio, representing the possibilities of rising above their lower instinctual nature into a higher state of awareness.

Seven: A number signifying the mind, knowledge, and self-awareness. This sacred number is seen in positions of importance throughout the known world: seven days of the week, seven visible colors of light, seven visible planets, and so on. In the major arcana, The Chariot (VII) carries the energy of the number seven.

Seventeen: A number reduced to eight (one plus seven) in numerology. This number combination signifies a crystallized vision or goal to be accomplished in the world and a vibration of success in accomplishing a clear intention. In the major arcana, The Star (XVII) carries the energy of the number seventeen.

Shadow: That which is not understood; an aspect of yourself that you may be unconscious about but is affecting you. A shadow may scare you, but it is not inherently negative. Facing your shadow brings gifts and greater self-awareness.

Shuffling: Mixing a deck of cards to change their order. Shuffling the Tarot is the process of blending your energy with the deck, thereby activating the principle of synchronicity. This is done so the cards you get in a reading offer the messages that are meant for you. You should shuffle as much or as little as feels right to you, though someone who is new to the deck should shuffle more thoroughly to fully merge their energy with it.

Signifier: An image, word, number, or symbol that points to a deeper meaning. Tarot is full of signifiers! Some are archetypal or universal, and others are subjective. Using your intuition can help you determine the signifier's meaning.

Six: A number that represents love, family, service, responsibility. Six is associated with the water element and feminine energy. In the major arcana, The Lovers card (VI) carries the energy of the number six.

Sixteen: A number reduced to seven (six plus one) in numerology. Sixteen is a powerful number combination that represents breakthroughs in consciousness and the ability to see how your thinking and your beliefs about yourself are limiting you. In the major arcana, The Tower (XVI) carries the energy of the number sixteen.

Source: A term used to mean the ultimate, all-pervading energy of the Universe—the unknowable, the alpha and the omega, that from which everything emerges. When you access your intuition or perform the "connect, ground, protect" exercise, you connect to Source. In Tarot, all higher guidance comes through your connection with Source energy.

Spiritual: Used generically to mean all that is related to religious, mystical, and esoteric study and practice. In Tarot, you focus on the spiritual aspects of life rather than just the material to gain awareness of a higher perspective.

Spread: One of the various layouts of Tarot that give structure to a reading. Laying out the cards in a particular order and using a variety of placements allows you to obtain different levels and degrees of insight and messages.

Staff: A symbol found in Tarot that signifies autonomy and leadership. The Hermit (IX) has a staff (walking stick) that helps him navigate uncharted terrain.

Story: The narrative throughout a spread of Tarot cards, interpreted through the symbolism and placement of the cards.

Stream of consciousness: Allowing the mind to follow a continuous flow of intuitive perceptions without editing or analyzing the information.

Strength: A major arcana card (VIII) that represents courage and being able to access internal fortitude. Strength is often portrayed as a woman with a lion. This card tells you to follow your instincts and to keep moving toward a desired goal. Summon and trust your innate strength.

Structure: A term pertaining to the overall organization of the seventy-eight cards of Tarot: the sequence of twenty-two major arcana cards that reveal information about the soul's journey and the pattern of the four suits of the minor arcana, each of which includes cards numbered from ace to ten and four court cards.

Subconscious: The part of the mind you are unaware of but that influences your thoughts and feelings. Certain positions in Tarot spreads can reveal what's going on in your subconscious. You should also try to ensure that your subconscious beliefs and desires don't influence your interpretations of the cards—be sure to tap into your intuition (higher guidance) and remain as objective as possible.

Suit: A grouping of cards in Tarot, each of which represents an element in nature and has its own significance. Those include:

- Swords: air, thought
- Cups: water, emotion
- Pentacles: earth, material things
- Wands: fire, action

Sun: A major arcana card (XIX) that heralds a time of joy, contentment, and positivity. Also, a signifier of a happy relationship, innocence, trust, and seeing the world through new eyes. The Sun also rules the zodiac sign of Leo, a sign known for shining brightly.

Sun sign: The position of the sun in one of the twelve astrological signs related to but not in exact alignment with the twelve constellations. Your Sun sign gives you basic information about your overall nature. When someone asks what your sign is, they're referring to your Sun sign, but this is only one of the pieces of a complex birth chart. In astrology, those born within the season of a particular sign (their Sun sign) share a similar set of attributes.

Swords: A suit in the minor arcana that relates to the air element. Various processes of mental activity and thought are represented by the suit of Swords. This suit contains most of the so-called negative cards in Tarot, which can make a reader or querent fearful of it. But these cards offer the most helpful information. They show you which thoughts and beliefs are impacting your life and where you can make changes if you don't like the trajectory you see in a reading.

Symbolism: The use of images to carry a deeper meaning and represent particular qualities, such as a mountain symbolizing higher consciousness and enlightenment. This is a primary method for conveying and accessing information in Tarot.

Synchronicity: When things come together in a meaningful way. This term was first used by Carl Jung to describe meaningful coincidences connected by an unseen force that bring a sense of wonder. For example, you pull The Sun (XIX) in a one-card reading, then you see the number nineteen in multiple places that same day. The Universe seems to be telling you that your card is important, or that those moments when you see the number nineteen pertain to your reading.

Synthesis: Bringing together many distinct parts in a way that is cohesive. Synthesis refers to the process of making connections in a Tarot reading to unify the meanings of the cards and their placements.

. . . . *T*

Taurus: The second astrological sign of the zodiac, governing those born between April 20 and May 20. This earth sign is ruled by the planet Venus and represented by the constellation of Taurus (the Bull). Those born under this sign are stable and earthy, enjoy sensual pleasures, and value material security. They have a reputation for being stubborn and slow to change.

Temperance: A major arcana card (XIV) symbolizing the integration of opposites and bringing together the masculine and feminine aspects of your nature (yin and yang). It also represents the synthesis of thinking and feeling, a time of psychological inquiry and awareness. It encourages you to understand your own mind and emotions to bring harmony within.

Ten: A number reduced to one (one plus zero) in numerology. The new energy of one combines with the grace of zero to represent opportunity, good timing, and a favorable new beginning. In the major arcana, the Wheel of Fortune (X) carries the energy of the number ten.

Theme: The core message or subject of a Tarot card or spread. In a spread of cards, the central card shows the main theme of the reading.

Thirteen: A number reduced to four (one plus three) in numerology. Thirteen is a powerful number signifying transformation of structure. It tells you that some situation is ending so that another may begin. In the major arcana, Death (XIII) carries the energy of the number thirteen, which is that of change and not physical death.

Three: A number representing grace, harmony, social interchange, and creativity. In the major arcana, The Empress (III) carries the energy of the number three.

Three-card spread: A Tarot layout in which the first card, placed in the central position, indicates the main theme of the reading. The second card, placed to the left, represents the past, and the third card, placed to the right, represents the future. This gives you more information than a one-card reading but still offers simple and straightforward guidance. It allows you to see the current trajectory from your past to your present and future, offering you a chance to make changes.

Timing: The time in which a card's or spread's guidance will come to fruition. Trying to ascertain the timing of events when using Tarot or any other divination tool can be tricky. Time is fluid, and intuitive information is outside the normal bounds of space and time. Looking at the sequence of events laid out in the cards will help with a sense of timing, but the true timing will depend on many factors—including the choices you make.

Transformation: The process of undergoing deep change. The Death card (XIII) in Tarot signifies just such a process. Remember that energy cannot be created or destroyed; it can only change from one form to another.

Twelve: A number that reduces to three (one plus two) in numerology. It represents trusting your heart, letting go, and relaxing into a time of ease and grace. In the major arcana, The Hanged Man (XII) carries the energy of the number three.

Twenty: A number that reduces to two (two plus zero) in numerology. It represents coming to understand a relationship with a significant other.

Balance, diplomacy, and compromise will bring greater awareness. In the major arcana, Judgment (XX) carries the energy of the number twenty.

Twenty-one: A number that reduces to three (two plus one) in numerology. It represents completion, wholeness, and harmony between the different aspects of your life. In the major arcana, The World (XXI) carries the energy of the number twenty-one.

Twenty-two: A master number in numerology; called the "Master Builder." Reduced to four (two plus two) in numerology, this is a powerful number that represents setting up structures that provide a foundation to serve the highest good. Not coincidentally, there are twenty-two cards in the major arcana (numbered zero through twenty-one).

Two: A number signifying balance, receptivity, sensitivity, and a focus on a relationship with another person. The High Priestess (II) carries the energy of the number two.

22

. . . .

U

Underlying card: The Tarot card at the bottom of the deck after you've shuffled, cut, and reassembled the cards. This card can give you insight into the underlying message of a reading.

Universe: Alternative name for Source, the totality of intelligent energy that pervades all of the manifest world. This is what you tap into when you access your intuition and the energetic source of the higher guidance you receive in a reading.

Uranus: The seventh planet from the Sun, with an orbital period of eighty-four years. In astrology, Uranus rules the zodiac sign Aquarius and brings awakening, surprises, flashes of insight, freedom from limiting beliefs, and radical change when found in a birth chart.

V: The Roman numeral for the number five, used in the major arcana cards.

V spread: A layout of seven cards in Tarot that form a V shape. This spread is used to gain comprehensive awareness about a particular situation in your life. The card at the point of the V indicates the main guidance about the situation, while the other cards add more detail.

Venus: The second planet from the Sun, with an orbital period of approximately 225 days. Venus is named for the Roman goddess of love (Greek: Aphrodite). This planet rules the zodiac signs of Taurus and Libra and represents beauty, love, money, and enjoyment of earthly pleasures. Venus's sensual energy can be felt in the minor arcana's The Empress (III).

Virgo: The sixth astrological sign of the zodiac, governing those born between August 23 and September 22. This earth sign is ruled by the planet Mercury and associated with the Virgo constellation (the Maiden). People born under Virgo are practical, hardworking, detail-oriented, and good with their hands. Although many Virgos are natural healers, this sign has a reputation for being a bit finicky and critical.

Visconti-Sforza deck: A collection of incomplete sets of hand-painted cards from the 1400s used to play a called game called *Tarocco* (*Tarot* in English) that is on display at the Morgan Library Museum in New York City. The cards were commissioned by the Visconti family of Milan and are some of the oldest surviving Tarot cards in existence.

Wands: A suit in the minor arcana that's associated with the element of fire. Wands signify energy, enthusiasm, and action in a reading.

Water: The element signifying feelings, emotions, and intuition. The suit of Cups represents the water element. When Cups or water show up in a reading, they represent your emotional state. They can also signify personal relationships.

Water signs: The astrological signs of Cancer, Scorpio, and Pisces. Each of these three signs are deeply emotional, intuitive, and sensitive. However, the individual water signs experience and express themselves in different ways: Cancer with nurturing, Scorpio with intensity, and Pisces with compassion. The court cards in the suit of Cups correspond to people born under the water signs or an aspect of yourself related to the emotional realm. For example, the Queen of Cups calls you to be more open and loving.

Wheel of Fortune: A major arcana card (X). This card indicates opportunity, expansion, and fortuitous change regarding the circumstances that surround you. In a reading, this card heralds good news. Expect more activity and excitement in your world! The Wheel of Fortune is a positive indicator for increased business and/or a change of location.

Wisdom: Deeper than mere knowledge, wisdom is gained through insight, self-awareness, intuition, and experience.

Witnessing: A term used to describe the act of stepping back from a situation—detaching from your thoughts and experiences to simply observe them. Witnessing helps you find equanimity and greater awareness. When you witness your thoughts and emotions, you can detach from them or work through them to retain objectivity in a reading.

World: The final major arcana card (XXI), which represents the end of the journey that began with The Fool (0). It signifies coming full circle but with conscious awareness, wisdom, and true understanding of your circumstances. The World can also indicate being at one with the Universe and a completion of a major era in your life.

X

X: The Roman numeral for the number ten, used in the major arcana cards.

Y

Yang: The masculine energy of assertion, action, and outward expression (not restricted to the male sex).

Yin: The feminine energy of feeling, receptivity, and sensitivity to inner experiences (not restricted to the female sex).

Z

Zero: In numerology, the number representing the Divine. With no beginning and no end, zero symbolically encompasses all. It adds the message of blessings, grace, ease, and abundance to whichever number it accompanies. For example, twenty is reduced to two but still carries the energy of zero, so it signifies grace and awareness regarding a relationship with another. The Fool (0) carries the energy of the number zero.

Zodiac: In astronomy, the twelve constellations on the plane of the ecliptic (the pathway that the Sun and Moon travel around the Earth). In astrology, the seasonal signs of the zodiac begin with Aries at the spring equinox and end with Pisces at the end of winter. Each sign represents 30 degrees of the 360-degree zodiacal chart.

Index